"Kyle Strobel has studied and reflected deeply on how it is that people actually change. If you've ever wondered about this yourself, Kyle is talking about your questions. Read him and morph!"

—John Ortberg, pastor, Menlo Park Presbyterian Church

"This book's subtitle, *Jesus as a Way of Life*, sums up what should be the heartbeat and life breath of us all. I can only pray that many, many people will read this book. What is written within these pages is by far the most important thing followers of Jesus can focus on, both for our own spiritual formation and for the collective health of the church at large. May we really pay attention to the wisdom within."

—Dan Kimball, author, *The Emerging Church*

"Kyle deconstructs some of our assumptions about the Bible, God's Spirit, and Christ's community in thought provoking ways. But he doesn't stop there; he rebuilds a thoroughly biblical understanding that adds rich texture to living conformed to the image of Christ."

—John Burke, author, *No Perfect People Allowed*

"Kyle Strobel's vulnerability drew me into *Metamorpha*. He is one who has struggled within the seeker sensitive church, who has wondered if conversion is the pinnacle of Christianity, and who longs to understand his part in spiritual change. He will guide you beyond your conversion experience into spiritual transformation itself. *Metamorpha* is a clarion call to the church to stop and evaluate our bumper-sticker, bullet-pointed, statistics-driven Christianity. If you are curious about becoming more like Christ, then *Metamorpha* deserves your careful attention."

—Jonalyn Fincher, cofounder of Soulation; author, *Ruby Slippers How the Soul of a Woman Brings Her Home*

"Kyle Strobel is a man deeply in touch with his peers. Accordingly, *Metamorpha* is full of stories, concerns, hopes, and suggestions that are right on the money for the emergent church generation. But Strobel is a man whose maturity of thought and life is far ahead of his years. With an honest heart and a hunger from God; graduate work in philosophy, spiritual formation, and New Testament studies; and a desire to impact the world for Jesus, Strobel provides deep insights for spiritual and church transformation. The tone of *Metamorpha* is neither preachy and condescending nor trivial and simplistic. Rather, it is an honest, accessible, straight-shooting examination of the human hunger for transformation and the way forward to authentic change. I was moved and encouraged by reading this book."

—J. P. Moreland, distinguished professor of philosophy, Biola University; author, *The Kingdom Triangle*

"Kyle brings together three hot topics—spiritual formation, unspoken worldviews, and authentic community—to provide a much-needed way forward for the evangelical church."

—Jan Johnson, author, *When the Soul Listens* and *Spiritual Disciplines Bible Studies*

"In *Metamorpha: Jesus as a Way of Life*, Kyle Strobel details how it is possible for believers to get past the rhetoric of our evangelical heritage and into the heart and soul of a lived Christian experience. Kyle's thinking on each topic—worldview change, a biblically formed lifestyle, the nature and role of community, and so on—goes deep and demonstrates an unusual and refreshing combination of theological insight and heartfelt devotion to Jesus Christ. The essentials of a well-rounded spiritual life that honors God and is likely to speak to the world in which we live is here in *Metamorpha*."

—Chuck Smith Jr., coauthor, *Frequently Avoided Questions*

"Kyle, a gifted storyteller with a mature Christian voice, leads us to intersecting crossroads where we must choose to live with our blind spots or move into wisdom. He takes us on a remarkable journey of looking deep within our individual and church-going lives."

—Katie Brazelton, author, *Pathway to Purpose*

METAmorpha

METAmorpha

Jesus as a way of life

kyleSTROBEL

BakerBooks

Grand Rapids, Michigan

© 2007 by Kyle Strobel

Published by Baker Books
a division of Baker Publishing Group
P.O. Box 6287, Grand Rapids, MI 49516-6287
www.bakerbooks.com

Printed in the United States of America

Library of Congress Cataloging-in-Publication Data
Strobel, Kyle, 1978–
    Metamorpha : Jesus as a way of life / Kyle Strobel.
      p.   cm.
    Includes bibliographical references.
    ISBN 10: 0-8010-6773-1 (pbk.)
    ISBN 978-0-8010-6773-0 (pbk.)
    1. Christian life. I. Title.
    BV4501.3.S783 2007
    248.4—dc22   2006039836

To Kelli—
My wife, friend, and companion for the journey.
Thank you for loving me
through the process of writing a book,
and
thank you that so much
of what you have given me
is on these pages.

I find two fundamentally divergent attitudes
among good people when they are faced with the
    unexaggerated,
yet undiluted gospel message.
One is exuberant enthusiasm.
The other is an "interpretation"
that reduces the message to a predictable
and merely human word.

—Thomas Dubay

CONTENTS

ACKNOWLEDGMENTS

Writing a book often feels a lot like pulling a piece of your heart out and trying to write with it. It is never just words on pages or sporadic ideas written down; it is a written testimony to what you have given yourself and your life. Because of this, there are several people who have been a part of my life and have helped model this for me, as well as encouraging and admonishing me in the process. My wife, Kelli, has been more than just an encouragement; she has been an editor, a critic, and a crutch to help carry me. She has been such a great partner for the journey, and every day I am more excited to live it out with her.

My mother and father have been supporters, encouragers, and guides through my entire life, and particularly during this project. It will never cease to amaze me how much they have supported me, even when doing so made no sense. My sister and brother-in-law (with Abigail's help of course), have helped work on the edits and drafts, many of which were painful to read. Like Kelli, they bore the burden of reading the earliest stuff! Baker Books as a whole has been a huge encouragement, but I want to note specifically my friend and editor at Baker, Chad Allen, who has been a huge support and an incredible editor as well. Chad did much more than merely help tweak this project; he really helped form it in a way I never could have alone. Likewise, my friend Don Pape was the reason this project "got legs," and he has been a cheerleader, supporter, and driving force for it. This book wouldn't have been nearly as fun as it was without him!

Because of how central my friends have been in my life, their devotion, love, and overall friendship have left their mark on these pages as well. Jamin Goggin, who has read for me, dialogued with me, and partnered with me on www.metamorpha.com, has walked through life with me through hard times and has allowed me to be honest and open in doing so, and I am grateful to his wife, Kristin, for letting me have him! My in-laws have supported me and my crazy schedule and have helped encourage me through this long process. My friends Brandon and Laurale (and of course Cole, Keaton, and Carter), George, Rob, Kent, Tim and Jamie, Norm, Aaron, Robby, Charles, Dubbs, my ISF brothers and my ISF family, my home group, and Fire, have all proven to be family to me in a way I have never thought possible. I would also like to thank the skeptics who have always been close to my heart and continually keep me questioning—Avy, Wade, and Joey—who will always be my brothers. My hope is that you will find in this book a journey into the unknown.

For all those who are a part of my life, named and un-named, I am so completely humbled that I have people like you to journey with. This book says much more about what you have taught me and modeled for me and about how you have loved me than it does about my own insights. I am grateful to you for being such a blessing in my life.

INTRODUCTION

Where I Write From

I am a child of the seeker church. Mine is probably the first generation of children whose parents became Christians in the seeker movement. The first time I sang a hymn was in college. I have been saved from facing issues that come with growing up around a lot of tradition; for example, I have no qualms with redoing everything if that is what is needed. On the other hand, my lack of tradition has left me feeling my way in the dark even though millions of others have walked the way before me. What I have always tried to take away from this odd tension, though, is that people take precedence over programs and models. Just as the Sabbath was made for man and not the other way around, so are church models and traditions. But as I've experienced personally and witness continually, the church often allows structure and tradition to segregate, disenfranchise, and alienate, even when those structures and traditions are only a couple of years old.

I want to see something different in my lifetime.

I am also a child of evangelicalism and went through the motions this movement said were necessary to be a leader. Yet I am a child of the emerging church as well, whose complaints and frustrations have been with me since childhood. Like so many of my generation, I have an abundance of frustrations and hurt from the church at large, but I cannot for the life of me give up on her.

I grew up thinking I was *in*, which was all that was really important to me. For people who have lived painful and scandalous lives, finally being *in* means a lot. For me, it meant little. I grew up in the church and was a reasonably good kid. *What was I saved from?* It seemed to me I was saved from God by God. I failed to see I was saved by God *for* God and that his saving grace means eternal living here and now.

My understanding of the Christian life had everything to do with what eventually will happen and had little to do with what currently is happening. I had walked through the door of Christianity, and I thought now my job was just to be a good person until Jesus came back. By God's grace I have learned there is much more. It's par for the course that, when we become Christians, we do so under many false pretenses and affirm things we don't remotely understand—as we will see, that's okay. But we must never fail to actually *journey with Jesus*. We have been saved that we may live the kingdom life *now*.

I want to show that we do not so much need an overview of what it means to be good as we do an invitation to journey with God. In North America, we have more often been a group of people who talk about all that Jesus came to do without any idea what it means for our lives now. It is my hope that we can journey together in search of greater meaning. Fortunately, we have a God who is gracious enough to equip us for the journey we have before us.

INVITATION

The Journey of Metamorpha

A student finishes his last class of seminary. Years of dedication and hard work have brought him to this glorious moment. The graduate is now presumed ready and qualified to shepherd a flock. He is destined to be the leader of souls.

On graduation day our student has an unusual run-in with one of the resident theologians. This particular theologian, well established in career and stoic in appearance, seems troubled as he approaches the student. "Ready for graduation?" the professor asks.

"Yeah!" responds the student, suspecting the professor has something else on his mind.

"May I ask you a question?" the professor asks.

"Sure," he answers, mentally thumbing through what he can remember of the prof's class.

"How do people change?"

The question sends the student's gaze into the sky; this is not a question about some obscure piece of doctrine. "What do you mean?"

"Change. How do people change?"

The student replies, "I have no idea."

This story, which has circulated for years, makes an important point: It is no wonder Christians have a limited effect on the world when, after three or more years of training, church leaders have not considered the question of how people change. While we understand full-well the Word as theology, the Word as a tool for transformation eludes many.

Why is change important? Why should we care about personal transformation? Well, for one thing, most of us need to change. In fact, if you think you're Christlike enough right now, this book is probably not for you. But most of us recognize the gap between who we are and who God made us to be.

This book is an invitation to transformation—*metamorpha*, as the Greeks used to say. It is about a willingness to change our minds, our perspectives, and our vision of life, because how we see affects who we are and who we will become.

Many Christians have been told that information leads to transformation and that all we need to do is download the right data into our heads and we will become Christlike. I hope to show that the process of transformation is more like a journey than a data download. And it's a journey worth taking—a journey of growth, discovery, risk, and new heights. It is, in fact, nothing less than the journey of following Christ.

Part 1

METAmorpha

A New Way of Seeing

1

OUR NEED

A New Way of Seeing

In the seventh grade I had an experience I'll never forget: God gave me a message. I can't prove it, nor can I even explain why I believe this, but to this day I would swear on it. I didn't really hear anything, but I was given a new reality. God called me to devote my life to ministry.

Toward the end of my senior year of high school, I was still suppressing that call. I was planning to go to school for electrical engineering until one day I was hit again with the profound realization that it was all wrong. I was taken back to that moment five years earlier and knew I had to submit. It wasn't easy, but once I did, I took a journey that helped make sense of that experience in the seventh grade. It was as if I had to walk forward before I could understand why walking forward was important.

Sometimes we need a new way of seeing.

Years later I looked back on my experience and wondered why I struggled to hear God's voice and calling in my life. I came to see it was because I held so tightly to my own perspective, my own idea of how the world worked, that nothing else could get in. My idea of the Christian life was going to church, doing good things, and trying to be nice. I always did the right "Christian" things. You know the type. I was in the "right" small group in the "right" church, involved in all the "right" ways. Meanwhile my faith, once a living thing, had grown stagnant and almost died. It was not until I let go of my perspective that my faith began to live again.

Sometimes we need a new way of seeing.

Cassie had an experience that was similar to mine. She recalls the struggle she had in seminary when she was reintroduced to God: "I remember crying silently in the back row in several classes as I watched in horror the God that I knew and loved being smashed to pieces as professors unwittingly dismantled my image of God, blow after painful blow." A professor who understood and related to Cassie's experience offered a story he thought might help her. In Cassie's own words:

> I will never forget the moment Professor Ray Anderson captured this experience with a story that eased my pain. He told his systematic theology class about a woman who, in her later years of life, decided to begin playing the piano. She searched for the best piano teacher she could possibly find and asked him how she could become a master pianist such as himself. He looked hesitantly at her, asking her if she was sure she

wanted to do this. He explained to her that at her age, the woman's bones had naturally calcified and were configured in a certain way. To play the piano, she would need to engage in finger exercises that would break this calcium down, thereby giving her supple, flexible fingers that would allow her fingers to extend to the various keys. He warned her that the finger exercises and the calcium breakdown would be excruciatingly painful, as if her fingers were being smashed.[1]

Sometimes we ignore our need for a new way of seeing.

Cassie soon realized that her spiritual calcification was being broken down. Because of her presuppositions, Cassie needed not only to *learn about* God but also to *unlearn what she falsely believed* about God. Cassie, like many others, believed that she could just tack on new information about God to what she already had. Unfortunately, what we erroneously believe about God is often solidified and unyielding, so it is painful to break down.

More often than not we choose against decalcification. We choose instead to talk about other Christians as the "them" and "those" who think differently. We isolate ourselves within a world of our own making.

Sometimes we ignore our need for a new way of seeing.

History tells of a man from Israel named Cleopas who walked with his friend on the road to a village called Emmaus. In grief over the loss of the one they thought would be their leader, the two men relate the news to a stranger: "We were hoping that it was he who was going to redeem Israel," Cleopas says. The stranger responds oddly, telling them how foolish they are for not believing the prophets. Later, at dinner, the stranger breaks bread, and the two men see for the first time that he is their Jesus, their King, their Savior. And Jesus disappears.

Sadly, we very often find ourselves on the same road; we might as well be looking Jesus in the face, but we cannot see him through our limited perspective. Let us hope and pray for the same moment of recognition that Cleopas and his friend experienced.

VISION OF LIFE

We all have a vision of life—a worldview—that helps us to explain reality and make value judgments. This vision becomes a story that we tell ourselves and others, either explicitly or implicitly.[2] The businessman who works seventy hours a week and says things like "time is money" and "knowledge is power" is telling a story about the way the world is. His life is a demonstration of his vision of reality. As we'll see, this vision of life serves as a kind of filter, letting in some bits of information and screening out others. This filter works on the level of instinct and intuition, below consciousness. We are seldom aware of it at all, just as people who wear eyeglasses eventually forget they're wearing them.

The priorities and beliefs that shape worldview are often so fundamental to who we are that we would never think of questioning them. Likewise, the beliefs we come to have about who we are, what Christianity is, and what the "good life" is all stem directly from our vision of life.

Several years ago I was planning to buy a car. As I was car searching on the Internet, my eyes landed on the new Nissan Altima. I had yet to see one in person, but I really liked how it looked. You can probably imagine what happened next. I started seeing them everywhere. It's not because there were more Altimas than there used to be, of course, but because my mind started seeking them out. Our minds naturally and subconsciously highlight objects and ideas that we have made a priority and screen out the ones we're not interested in, which is why Honda Civics and Land Rovers failed to catch my eye.

Here's a rather overblown example of how this could work out in a Christian's life. Let's imagine the Gospel Church of Akron has been having a potluck dinner every year for the past fifty years on December 24 to bring in Christmas day. But one year the church is asked by a desperate homeless shelter to serve a dinner to poor folks that evening. Most of the church is more than willing, but there is a small group of people who make a fuss and complain that, "Without the Christmas Eve potluck, it just won't feel like Christmas." Too often we have subconsciously solidified the Christian life and have failed to ask questions about whether we are upholding the biblical ideal. Just as I started seeing Altimas on the road, we often call things "Christian" only when they fit into our preconceived notions and experiences.

We can see this play out in all sorts of ways: How often do Christians think so much of their style of worship that they begin to think it is the only right way to worship? How often do churches become so much like corporations that if a staff member suggested meeting just to socialize, other staff would see it as a waste of time? How often does a leader within a church become so well-respected that what he or she says is always taken as gospel truth?

The list of possible examples is endless, and worldviews work on such a subtle level that the above examples still seem too obvious. Think of Cassie and her difficulty picturing God differently from how she had always thought of him. Think of me and my routine way of viewing how Christians ought to live. Think of Cleopas on the road to Emmaus.

In many cultures a whole people or tribe will have a common vision of life that is passed on, held up, and defended by generations. In North America, by contrast, we have lifted up the individual and his or her own view. The U.S., then, is a whole nation of people telling the individual stories they see fit and living as if their own personal views of reality are complete.

Just as I didn't choose to start seeing Altimas, we do not choose what our view of reality will be. The situation in which we grow up, the time in history, and the kind of family and friends we have all determine the way we see reality. An adolescent male from inner-city Los Angeles and a male of the same age living just an hour south in Orange County will see the world in totally different ways. Not only will their values be different, they will have entirely different ways of interpreting the world.

We do not notice our own vision of life, but we can immediately detect when other people's vision and stories differ from ours, and we often find those differences offensive, wrong, or just plain weird. A telltale sign that you are speaking out of your own particular vision of life is when you critique someone by saying, "Well, that's just obvious!"

I can't emphasize enough how important this discussion is for Christians. Our Christianity can often look more North American and modern than distinctively Christian. Our churches often take their priorities and values directly from the society in which they exist and simply Christianize them. The story we are telling has everything to do with the worldview we have, and redeeming this worldview should be central to our lives as disciples.

Job: A Study in Blind Spots

In the biblical story of Job, we see three distinct visions of life functioning at once. Job's friends are convinced they understand what is going on. Their vision of life can explain the reality Job is experiencing, and they are convinced that they know why he is suffering. God must be punishing Job; there is no other explanation. Therefore, Job did something horribly wrong. It is obvious, simple, and cut-and-dried: The innocent do not suffer; sinners do.

Job, on the other hand, does not believe he has done anything deserving of the torture that in his mind has clearly come from God. He, as much as his friends, takes a very arrogant stance about what the world is like. Neither Job nor his friends back down in their debates; their visions of life will not let them.

The third vision of life is God's. What Job and his friends fail to see, but what the reader knows, is that God is allowing the torture but is not causing it to happen. Interestingly, God never feels it is important to let them know this but instead lets them know that his story is *the* story. Somehow it is enough to let them know that his story takes precedence over theirs. Their views are narrow and without understanding, while God's is as vast as the starry heavens.

Often it seems we can find ourselves speaking out of our vision of life as if we have infinite knowledge. When we fail to take seriously our inevitable naiveties, we may find ourselves under God's rebuke, even when we thought we were defending him.

An older friend of mine tells a story about people from the church of his childhood. That generation, most of whom have since died, sought God and his decrees and yet still believed black people were of less value than white people. For some reason the story of life they told did not notice the reality that racism is wrong.

It is easy for us to look back and shake our heads, arrogantly thinking that we don't have similar blind spots in the stories we tell. Yet C. S. Lewis suggests otherwise and tells people that they should read old books so that they can begin to see these blind spots:

> The Christian life is not living out how we already see; it is a journey of redemption.

Every age has its own outlook. It is specially good at seeing certain truths and specially liable to make certain mistakes. . . . Nothing strikes me more when I read the controversies of past ages than the fact that both sides were usually assuming without question a good deal which we should now absolutely deny. . . . We may be sure that the characteristic blindness of the twentieth century—the blindness about which posterity will ask, "But how could they have thought that?"—lies where we have never suspected it.[3]

In the story of Job as well as in the racist church, we see the reality in which we find ourselves. We often fail to see our vision of life as something that needs to be changed. We are Job's friends, confident in our viewpoint and beliefs, not needing advice or humility.

The Christian life is not living out how we already see; it is a journey of redemption. We have a way of seeing reality, a story we are telling, and the way we live reveals that viewpoint and story. When we allow our story to stagnate and fail to see the Christian life as a continual process of growth, we come to God demanding *our* way and do not take *his* way seriously.

A Directional Lens

When I was in high school, I brought a Catholic friend to my youth group. This friend, who really didn't want anything to do with religion, had never been to an evangelical service. His understanding of church was almost entirely formed by his experience of growing up attending Catholic Mass. The first thing he said as we pulled out of our parking place was, "That wasn't church." What he experienced in a room with a couple hundred high school students could not possibly qualify as "church," at least not according to the story of reality he had been told and now was telling.

Our vision of life is more than just the way we naturally see the world. It "tells us both what is (and is not) the case and what ought (and ought not) to be the case," says James Olthuis. "A worldview is both a sketch of and a blueprint for reality; it describes what we see and stipulates what we should see."[4] In this sense, our vision of life is a *directional* lens; it tells us, rightly or wrongly, how the world should be.

In the modern period, our culture championed Enlightenment values (empiricism, "unbiased reason," the scientific method, and so on), so that today the church is comprised of several generations of people who think more or less like scientists. The story told during the Enlightenment was one that had a very high regard for the ability of humans to discern reality objectively. The church followed suit by making information transmission the highest good, the way people grew.

Many Christians today have an entrenched, Enlightenment way of understanding what church is and isn't—of what the Christian life is and isn't. And if church does not fit within these parameters, they are likely to say, "That wasn't church." We have a story in our minds of what it means to live as a Christian, and that is the way we try to live. But what if this is one of the blind spots that C. S. Lewis was talking about? I tend to think it is.

It may sound strange, but I believe much of Jesus's ministry was about worldview development. The disciples had a very solidified understanding of what the kingdom would be like (political, military, religious) and what sort of judgment God would bring down on people who would not submit to the king. At one point Jesus sent messengers ahead to make preparations for his travels among the Samaritans. The Gospel of Luke tells us that the Samaritans would not accept him. In response, James and John asked Jesus, "Lord, do You want us to command fire to come down from heaven and consume them?" (Luke 9:54). With this question the disciples revealed the story they lived by, but Jesus rebuked them, indicating starkly that he lived by a very different story.

While we rarely ask God to bring fire down on people, we often do things that are equally absurd. We split churches, disenfranchise those who don't agree with us, or ignore the problems in the church to focus on sin outside the church. Like James and John, our visions of life shape our expectations, and our actions flow out of that vision. I know of evangelical churches located within blocks of other evangelical churches that would not give one another the time of day, let alone share in the work of ministry.

Rigor Mortis of the Eyes

For many Christians, the call Jesus issues to repent and believe in him has much more to do with conversion than with life after conversion. We see conversion as a door we walk through and Christian life as solidified and complete. Once you're saved, you are to fulfill the tasks of the church.

In other words, Christians often become cheap labor for the movements they believe in.

This paradigm is a story Christians tell the world through the way we live. It also serves as a lens for looking at the world—a lens that is fixed and unchanging. Oftentimes this lens is developed through childhood. It is the result of upbringing, religion, experience, education, and so on.

We all have beliefs that are so deeply embedded in our worldview that we would never even think to doubt them. Say you enter a room and a ball is floating in midair. Is your first thought that you have been wrong about gravity? Probably not. You are more likely to believe you're seeing an optical illusion or something peculiar about the ball or the room. Why? Because gravity has always made sense in the past. Why shouldn't it now? Note how one's belief about gravity may seem like an insignificant detail most of the time. So then the question becomes: When would the theory of gravity come up for reconsideration? What would it take for you to be willing to abandon your belief in it? How about when it comes to your faith: What about the idea that the gospel is only about conversion? What about the idea that there is such a thing as the "best" way to worship? What would it take for you to be willing to rethink these kinds of ideas? My point is that the rigidity of one's vision of life is determined by how long one holds onto beliefs when everything around that person seems to say they are false. Oftentimes, when our lens is called into question, our response is to hold onto our presuppositions even tighter and move on.

> Christians often become cheap labor for the movements they believe in.

We *should* have some beliefs that hold strong against critique. (Abandoning the idea of gravity is, in most cases, not a wise thing to do.) But we must not allow our way of looking at reality to permanently set, and this is just what many of us have been taught to do. We stop at sentences of dogma downloaded to us from some kind of "authority"—usually a book, an experience, a parent, or a pastor—and we let it turn to concrete in our minds.

When I was in seminary, we often had extended conversations about biblical passages. On many occasions, particularly when we were looking into the Jewish background of a passage that shed new light on its meaning, a student would fight against the teacher as if the student's Christian experience were being undermined by the different interpretation being presented by the teacher. Our worldview can become so inflexible that we see our personal views about the Bible as authoritative and certain, and we regard any new or different information as dangerous and wrong. Sadly, what we call "faith" is more like self-trust because it is rooted in our ability to wrap our minds around the things of Christianity and is not oriented toward God himself. In the Gospels we see Jesus running into the same thing. People could hear but could not understand; they could see but not truly perceive because Jesus did not fit into the Jewish worldview of the day.

We're faced with a choice when our worldview is challenged: we can remain humbly open to the possibility for worldview deconstruction, or we can throw up barricades. The Christian can admit that the story she believed was naive and recognize that she, like everyone else, will never have absolute interpretive certainty, or she can protect herself by holding white-knuckled onto her story and ignoring the new information.

One of the many lessons we should learn from the Jewish authorities in the ancient world is that it is dangerous when our eyes are drawn to our own systematic understanding of what following God looks like. The Pharisees had their eyes so fixated on not breaking Torah that they failed to follow God. Their mistake was to make an end out of what should have been a means. We sometimes make the same mistake.

The longer we live as Christians, the easier it becomes to have rigor mortis of the eyes—to solidify our presuppositions about the Christian life so that we only see the text of the Bible through our worldview. In this way, to a very real degree, we fail to see the text at all. When this happens, the Bible can become a series of "acceptable," "offensive," "defensive," and "problematic" passages. The Word stops living and becomes a book of proof-texts for our own personal argumentation.

An easy answer to these worldview problems might be, "Do not let your worldview get in the way of reality," or "Stop systematizing things!" But the issue runs much deeper than that. Certain things need to be systematized; avoiding systems would be another overreaction for a church that is well known for overreacting! We need a way to journey well and not merely wander under the blindness of our own desires and assumptions.

LOOKING AHEAD

The Christian life is a life of increasing sight; the story we tell has to allow for the fact that on a journey, the farther down the road we travel, the more we see. Our growth depends on seeing anew.

Maybe you have seen the image of two identical profiles looking at each other, with a white space in between them. Suddenly, though, when you focus on the space between them, you cease to see the profiles and see a vase instead. This shift in sight is referred to as a *gestalt shift*. In the Christian life we will have many gestalt shifts, some drastic (conversion) and many not so drastic. Cassie wept in the back of her classroom because she felt the pain of a worldview shift. Cleopas and his friend had their entire reality reoriented because the King whom they presumed dead was among them. Their vision took a dramatic shift, and now the world they lived in was a different place.

In our context, then, we need something more than a five-step (or three-step or seven-step) program to discipleship, growth, and development. We need an entirely new way to engage with reality—one that refrains from arrogance and seeks God for redemption. The Christian life is a journey of redemption, a developmental process of growth. Our visions of life should constantly be changing and re-forming; the enemy of a healthy faith is a worldview that is static and "complete." We need a way to undergo gestalt shifts when necessary so that we may have our vision renewed and developed according to God's story and not merely our own.

2

OUR HOPE

Embracing Metamorpha

Throughout most of my life I was consumed with finding all the right answers, being a part of the right church, and even joining the right movement. Many other Christians I knew were the same way. Can you relate? Eventually, I came to realize that I needed to befriend my Creator, who was constantly trying to befriend me.

Merely *doing* church in a new way or deconstructing all of the structures that we think are hindering us will not help us get closer to God. There is room for those things, but our task has to be more fundamental: we have to be about becoming something new. I believe this involves seeing the world in a new way.

A lot can be learned about the church's current worldview by examining the way it has neglected the Christian life as a developmental journey. As a culture we avoid anything

> Merely *doing* church in a new way or deconstructing all of the structures that we think are hindering us will not help us get closer to God.

that requires a lengthy commitment of our time; we want our food fast, our dieting easy, and our entertainment now. We think we can get what we need by acting like the stereotypical detective, functioning on *the facts and nothing but the facts*. Not only does this approach fail to take reality seriously, but it fails to take seriously the reality that Jesus wants to walk with us, teach us, and show us around his kingdom. That requires an investment of emotion and time.

Consider a passport. By itself, a passport is not likely to change the way you see the world, but if you're willing to invest some time and effort, it could enable you to take a journey to distant lands and experience things that have the potential to reshape your lens, your worldview. Conversion is the spiritual version of a passport. With it we are offered a portal to a new world, but it is only if we take advantage of this portal that we can come to see the world in a new way.

We have to commit to the journey.

METAMORPHA: THE LENS OF CHANGE

For many Christians, conversion has never been a portal to a way of life involving change and seeing a new reality. Life is filled with doing "Christian" things but never really growing into a deeper love for and union with Christ. Because of this lack of change and growth, people continually find the Christian life stagnant, boring, and irrelevant. But this wasn't the life Jesus offered.

By seeing conversion as a passport to a life-changing adventure, we have a way to journey well, a way I call *metamorpha*. *Metamorpha* is the Greek word meaning "transformation," from which we get our word *metamorphosis*, describing one of the more radical transformations seen in nature. The *metamorpha* life is one of continual deconstruction and reconstruction of our views. It grows out of an understanding of God's unwavering desire to redeem us and not leave us as we are. The *metamorpha* life is the life of which Jesus called us to count the cost by asking, "Are we really open to seeing the world in the way God has called us to see it?"

A life lived the *metamorpha* way is analogous to the life lived by a person who walks away unscathed from a massive car wreck. Colors are brighter, the air is crisper, and time seems more substantial because all of life is now lived from the reference point of near-death. For the Christian living a life of *metamorpha*, death has already been lived. In the words of Paul, "I have been crucified with Christ; and it is no longer I who live, but Christ lives in me" (Gal. 2:20). This is where the journey begins.

Opposing the life of *metamorpha* is the life of *staticus*. *Staticus* is a Latin word from whose root comes the word *static*. To live the *staticus* life is to avoid the reality that we have assumptions and presuppositions. It is an easy temptation for those who have been in Christian circles for a long time to believe their personal view of the world is "fully Christian," even though they can oftentimes offer little reason for believing so. But taking the journey of *metamorpha* is to realize that God is much bigger than our assumptions and presuppositions, whatever they are, and that our role is to open ourselves to having them reformed.

The kind of life we see in Paul's missionary letters and in the teaching of Jesus is a life of formation. In their teachings it is understood that we come to God just as we come to everything else—with a lot of baggage. This is why it is so important to recognize that we're on a journey of opening and submitting to the work of God to inform and nurture our growth. The role of one's worldview, then, should be one of counsel, not one that is unbendingly definitive.

The role of one's worldview, then, should be one of counsel, not one that is unbendingly definitive.

While we probably never enter any dialogue without presuppositions, we do in fact have control over the majority of them. Cassie, whose story we read earlier, sat crying in the back of her classroom because she allowed her view of God to be critiqued. Instead of coloring her professor's comments to match her worldview, she opened herself up to being wrong. In so doing she felt the pain the disciples felt as their view of reality was turned upside down.

By embracing *metamorpha*, the story to which we are giving ourselves will vary in how concrete and perfected it is. There will still be plenty of things that are not up for debate—such as the fact that Jesus is the Messiah—and those things will become more and more central to how we see the world. In the same way that a wedding inaugurates the journey of two people growing together into deeper love, conversion is a gateway to a life of deeper and deeper love, trust, and devotion to the Redeemer. To continue the comparison, if we are not open to having our assumptions and presuppositions about marriage deconstructed, our ability to grow in love and develop as a spouse will be hindered and thwarted. In the same way, our spiritual growth is hindered and thwarted if our presuppositions include exactly how Jesus will and will not act in our lives, and if those presuppositions are never brought into question. We need to be open to telling a new story, and that is exactly what Jesus came to help us do.

When confronted with the reality that our worldview may be maligned and naive, we might be tempted to deny that we're wrong or else lose faith that we are right about anything at all. However, there is a middle ground. This is where we realize we *do* have worldview presuppositions but that they can be transformed. Jesus assumes that his followers bring worldview baggage to the religious table, but in his message to "Follow me" he requires his followers to hand over their worldviews for deconstruction.

It is essential to recognize that Christianity is based upon actual events within history. These events require proper interpretation within their context and against the culture of the day in which they occurred, which will often lead to a change in a facet of our worldview lens. The commands and values in Christianity are always grounded in something true about reality (resurrection, judgment, sin, etc.), which is what makes right "seeing" extremely important. Faith is having the ability to "see" spiritually what we cannot see physically (Heb. 11:1). We need a way to grow in our ability to see spiritually.

The path of *metamorpha* will always include means such as programs, spiritual disciplines, and church services. Those are not the problem. The problem is that we end up, in practice, placing more importance on the means as opposed to the end: a relationship with Jesus. The programs that we do enact and the disciplines we take part in will serve as windows into our worldviews that point to the deeper reality of what our actual vision of life is.

To return to an earlier illustration, the person who faithfully renews his passport but never travels abroad tells a story

The problem is that we end up, in practice, placing more importance on the means as opposed to the end: a relationship with Jesus.

about his view of the world. It is a story of being forever prepared for a trip that will never happen. In the same way, those whose lives remain significantly unchanged after conversion fail to walk with God. They have the passport to a renewed life with the Lord, but their faith never goes anywhere, showing us that they believe conversion to be the end-all experience of the Christian life. But we're not converting to a cause or an ethic; we're converting to a relationship that should (and will, if we travel well) change everything.

Yet our goal in deconstructing our worldview is not to change things arbitrarily just for the sake of change but to question whether we have arrogantly solidified that which we find comfortable.[1] Jesus asks converts to count the cost, which includes having their stories changed. Likewise, we need to ask if we are so comfortable in the story we are telling that we refuse to hear another. If we affirm that the Christian life is developmental, we must be willing to walk the path for growth to which Jesus calls us. An essential part of that growth will be accepting a worldview that is open for developmental journeying with the Spirit. If it isn't, we will find ourselves dry, unfulfilled, and frustrated with the Christian life.

THE INFORMERS

A passport isn't enough to be a world traveler; if we're to have a good journey, we need, among other things, money, a plane, a place to stay, and a final destination. Just as we should not show up at the airport without these other things in mind, we should not wander through the Christian life unequipped. God comes alongside us to provide the equipment we need so that we may have a good journey learning and growing under his direction.

> This is the equipment you'll need for the *metamorpha* journey: the Bible, the Spirit, and community.

This is the equipment you'll need for the *metamorpha* journey: the Bible, the Spirit, and a community of believers to travel with. I like to call these the "informers" because they are the tools Jesus uses to alter, or inform, our vision. Our vision is rarely radically changed all at once; it is usually altered and informed over time by these tools. Journeying well doesn't necessarily mean knowing the directions or understanding what it means to *walk*; it means being informed by the one who does know these things.

The importance of each of these informers can be seen by their prominence in Scripture as well as by the vast amount of literature Christians have written on them through the centuries. It is clear that the Bible, the Spirit, and community are essential elements for growth, both personal and communal. These are not the only worldview informers a Christian should have, of course, but they are necessary for proper and intentional development.

In the same way that our life tells a story about who we are and what we believe, our vision of life tells a story about what has informed our vision. In many cases we are informed at random, never thinking much about how we see the world. Paul ran into this scenario and wrote a letter to the church at Galatia because of it. A group of Jews there had plugged Jesus into their worldview but failed to have it informed by

Jesus's teaching. They wanted the moment of conversion without counting the cost of vision deconstruction. Likewise, it can be easy for us to plug Jesus into our North American worldview and then fail to take seriously his path for growth.

> The informers don't merely inform us; they help us to shape, tear down, and rebuild our views of reality.

The informers don't merely inform us; they help us to shape, tear down, and rebuild our views of reality. Just as dreaming of foreign lands won't make us world travelers, we can't merely think about or memorize facets of the Christian life that we do not live out. Experience is required for a true overhaul of our worldview. Change takes place because God walks with us and uses our experiences as means for growth.

Just as a gardener uses wire scaffolding to guide the process of growth for a vine, so the worldview informers guide our growth. There will be plenty of times we are trying to grow away from them, and there will be plenty of times that their pull and guidance hurt so much it is nearly impossible to see it as progress. But this is the reality of the Christian life: we are holistically deconstructed by the grace of God, and the tools God uses for this task are the Bible, the Spirit, and community.

To get a better sense of the specific uses of each informer, we can think of them in terms of a telescope. For a telescope to work well, three major things need to be in order: The telescope needs to be aimed rightly (Bible), focused well (Spirit),[2] and in the right environment to work (community).[3] A well-aimed and focused telescope in a fog doesn't get the job done, and having either the aim or focus "off" does not allow the telescope to function as it is designed to. Likewise, to journey well we need our eyes drawn to whatever horizon God has deemed worthy, and the worldview informers help to clarify and seek that end.

When someone takes care of his or her body by eating well, working out, and resting appropriately, we call that person "healthy." It is in this sense that we talk about a person being spiritually healthy as well. A healthy Christian is one who is open to the hand of the Potter, allowing him to mold and sculpt his or her life according to his plan. The healthy Christian life is not understood as complete or having arrived but in terms of journeying well, guided by the three worldview informers.

Unfortunately, more often we read the Bible *through* our worldview rather than allowing it to *inform* our worldview.

As travelers on a path, it is necessary to see well, grow in our knowledge of our environment, and be guided by travelers more experienced than ourselves. This is why the informers are so important. They give us a means of growth and formation which, when well-balanced, will lead to kingdom living.

Unfortunately, more often we read the Bible *through* our worldview rather than allowing it to *inform* our worldview. We often see our personal view as biblical, not because it is biblically informed, but because we have always assumed it to be. The task of *metamorpha* will be to open ourselves up to the work of God through his Word. As we will see, this task is only possible through the power of the Spirit within community.

In the same vein, the Spirit is often spoken of, but rarely related to. The "rivers of living water" that Jesus spoke of when referring to the Spirit (John 7:37–39) feel much more like fields of dust to many of us. The cry that has come to characterize my generation is, "There must be something more!" The Spirit is what seems to be missing from much of our conversation. As travelers along the way, the Spirit must become our inner-guide, the person who informs us from the inside out.

Our interaction with Jesus and the Spirit through the text of the Bible helps us to *know* in a more intimate sense, as one grows in knowledge of another person, rather than in a scientific sense, as one knows an object. But this knowledge can only truly be known in community. We bring too much baggage to the worldview table to engage it truthfully and fully on our own. Community acts as a mirror and as a counselor, reflecting back to us a reality that we may not see and critiquing us in ways we may not always appreciate.

Because our conversion was to a person, and therefore to a life of growing union with that person, our understanding of what religion is should be more dynamic than static. In the same way, someone who fails to see marriage as dynamic may fail to grow in love and may allow his or her love to grow more and more selfish and cold. Just as marriage vows might not say anything about the actual love between the couple, our vow of union must be followed with a life open to growth if it is to grow at all. In light of this, someone's ability to affirm that "Jesus is God" might not actually say anything about what he or she believes. This is the disconcerting reality that we must come face-to-face with personally and communally in the church today.

Typically we talk about the Bible, the Spirit, and community in static terms, framing them as tools that we use rather than living entities that have the power to change us through God's use of them on us. Also, we have a tendency to favor one informer over the others because we find it easier to relate to that one. Often you can look at the makeup of a church and know immediately what informer the pastor favors. The fundamentalists and most evangelicals focus on the Word, hint at community, and are virtually silent on the Spirit. Charismatic churches focus on the Spirit but often lose out on the Bible. "Liberal" movements have designed their mission around community but have relegated the Bible and the Spirit to a back burner. In our call for the universal church to be of one mind, we have been anything but, pointing fingers at each other because of the misuse of Scripture, the absence of the Spirit, or a lack of mercy.

The life of *metamorpha* starts with an understanding that the Christian life is developmental and progressive—a life with a person and not a life committed to a system. From there, this life understands that Jesus is about redeeming, and redemption means much more than what we do on Sunday mornings. It is a journey of belief transformation. Our call is for new sight, that the old may go and the new may come to life.

3

OUR REALITY

A Tale of Two Visions

When I was in college I became a resident advisor in my dorm. The RA position at my college, like most Christian schools, was not merely disciplinary but also carried an element of spiritual formation. I was supposed to be someone students could come to for guidance, prayer, or mentoring, no matter where they were on their journey with God.

While I was being trained for my position, I was told that if anyone comes to the school who is either not a Christian or does not know how to live according to the school's standards, they will tell them to look at me and live like I do. At the time, that was both the scariest and the most ridiculous thing I had ever heard. Although I was trying my hardest to live well, I was overwhelmed with my total inadequacy to do so.

I was alone in my dorm room one night, thinking about my life. In a rare moment of clarity, I came to the conclusion that I didn't believe that prayer worked. In the meditation that followed I had one of the most honest conversations with God I've ever had. I told him that I didn't believe he answers my prayers but that I wanted to change. *I believe; help my unbelief.*

I could have told you numerous stories about answered prayer, and I could recite a well-developed argument for the efficacy of prayer based on the Bible and church history. It wasn't that I suddenly realized I didn't believe in God—I most certainly did. My problem was that I didn't pray much. Finding out what you really believe is simple: look at your life. Where do you spend the most energy and time? What actions or practices make up your day? What's missing? Suffice it to say there is something profoundly self-contradictory about believing on the one hand that God hears and answers prayer and, on the other, simply not getting around to praying.

God was guiding me on a path I would walk for a long time. I came to realize that it is impossible to simply tell myself what I believe, because there are plenty of things I only think I believe. The only real way to determine my beliefs is to see how I live week in and week out. This is why the worldview conversation is so important. According to Brian J. Walsh and J. Richard Middleton, "World views are best understood as we see them incarnated, fleshed out in

> Finding out what you really believe is simple: look at your life.

actual ways of life. . . . World views are perceptual frameworks. They are ways of seeing. If we want to understand what people see, or how well people see, we need to watch how they walk."[1]

Looking back on my experience with prayer, I realize now that the Spirit was moving in my life. One of the major tools the Spirit used was the Bible. Even though I was struggling with the discontinuity between my life and the text, I was encouraged by how much my major in school—Biblical Studies—required me to be in the Bible. Because of that discontinuity I realized I didn't really believe as much about God as I thought I did. Intuitively, I got together with a group of friends and confessed this to them. To my surprise, they confessed back. It became our goal, in community, to live out a prayer life that was as vibrant as the one the Bible called us to.

Incidentally, it was only by the grace of God that I told anyone. The reason I did was because my unbelief hit me so hard I was scared to death. For the first time in my life I saw myself as I really was, not through a "Christian" lens. I typically just saw myself as forgiven, but now I saw myself as greedy, lazy, and unbelieving. I felt the burden of being a spiritual leader without being spiritual, someone who was wise without wisdom, and a person of depth who had just realized he didn't believe prayer works! I was a leader because that was the role I played, and I thought I knew how to play it well, but my leadership was skin-deep.

Until that moment I had never been able to visualize a three-dimensional picture of the Pharisees. They were always just these tall caricatures in robes who thought they could earn salvation. But then it hit me that I was a Pharisee—the whitewashed tomb of dead men's bones (see Matt. 23:27).

> I fear that our conversations in the church focus more on our bad fruit than on the fact that we are sick trees.

That moment is what led me to see I lived a secular life onto which I had slapped the label "Christian." I followed God on my terms, in my ways, and on my time.

One of Jesus's central word-pictures is that of a tree bearing fruit, either good or bad. Right after being confronted about my inability to believe in prayer, I was confronted with Jesus's idea of being a good tree. In Jesus's own words, "Every good tree bears good fruit, but the bad tree bears bad fruit. A good tree cannot produce bad fruit, nor can a bad tree produce good fruit" (Matt. 7:17–18). I realized that I hadn't been concerned if I was a good tree; all I cared about was whether it looked like I had good fruit. I had been taking bad and ugly fruit off of the tree, brushing some green paint on it to make it look good, and gluing it back on. I was failing to live by the central tenent of Jesus's teaching: "Without me you can do nothing" (see John 15:5).

I fear that our conversations in the church focus more on our bad fruit than on the fact that we are sick trees.

God has called us on a journey to live with him. He has given us a way to discern our bearings on the path so that we continue to grow and thrive. The worldview informers act as roots for the tree seeking life-giving water. If we attend to God through the Spirit, the Bible, and community and have our worldviews informed by those things, we will bear fruit according to the time and abundance that God has prepared. This is not a call to a new movement but to engage with God and his movement—to see the world as he would have us see it.

Our Reality vs. Our Hope

The worldview informers are not at all controversial, yet they are rarely engaged to the full. In our present situation, the typical Christian has very different worldview informers—and is encouraged to have them by the church! Instead of the Bible, the Spirit, and community, the typical North American Christian looks to self-help books to live a more gratifying existence, to their subjective feelings to check their spiritual temperature, and to their head pastor to tell them what to do.

Because this kind of development is not relational, it fails to engage people where they are and instead becomes "things to do to feel better." The way a person feels is often how the church and the act of communal worship are judged. The latest and greatest book serves to soothe the anxiety and explain the lack of growth, and Christians inevitably go from book to book and from praise service to praise service to appease their fickle feelings. In the end, a person will do a lot of so-called "Christian" things but will fail to engage reality Christianly.

The worldview informers that are currently in use tend to exacerbate the problem: we are a people who have never seen true biblical community, we often have no idea what to do with the Spirit, and our approach to growth differs little from that of the world. When we are honest, that is where we find ourselves. However, my examples have been stark contrasts, whereas things are not always as obvious as this. Much of our problem stems from an inability to see the problem in the first place.

Let's look at the differences of these two major worldviews and how they play out in reality. What does it look like to adopt a developmental/journeying model of the Christian life over against a solidified/"arrived" model? Several characteristics may help us to distinguish between these.

Solidified/*Staticus*	Developmental/*Metamorpha*
Bible is read through worldview.	Bible interacts with and critiques worldview.
Worldview change stops at assimilation.	Worldview change is the Christian life.
Christian instruction is data driven.	Christian instruction is belief driven.
Church is an institutional task.	Church is a relational task.
Discipleship is a call to right understanding.	Discipleship is a call to right "becoming."[2]
Church is focused on growth.	Church is focused on abiding in Christ.
Christianity is a door to walk through.	Christianity is a path to take.
The enemy is heresy.	The enemy is a lack of change.

It is important to note that these characteristics have an infinite number of degrees. It is best to see them as the two sides of a continuum rather than two hermetically sealed categories. Like our beliefs, the approach we take is made known by how we live or, in the case of a church, how it functions. To make these lists more lifelike, let's look at a brief sketch of each within the life of the church and the individual believer.

A SOLIDIFIED MODEL

A dead giveaway of a solidified-minded church is when the majority of the church's resources are allocated toward Sunday services in general and preaching in particular. The focus of these churches is on preaching because the pastor is (presumably) the one who has the requisite education and the *information* that the people need. The greatest "good" is to have churchgoers in contact with the pastor so they can receive the right *information*, since information downloading has become the goal and focus of pastoral ministry.

The highest goal of this kind of church is *right understanding*, and the greatest enemy is heresy, or wrong understanding. Right understanding becomes the utmost level of Christian discipleship. In light of this, the Sunday service is sacred territory for these churches. In these services, brothers and sisters in Christ meet and greet casually, returning to their seats to close their eyes and sing to God in isolation. Communion, if offered, is experienced in a similar way—as an individual and isolated event. The cut-and-dried, prepackaged message is mass-produced for a wide audience and is not so much taught as it is presented. All the bases sufficiently covered, the service concludes, and people return to their isolated lives. When the tree (i.e., the church) is recognized as having bad fruit, the answer is usually to fiddle with a branch (e.g., add a new staff position, start a new preaching series, add an interactive element to the service). In order to try and curb the lack of interest and the obvious lack of growth, programs are introduced. The church forms groups and offers classes in an attempt to make up for what the people are missing. Unfortunately, people tend to learn facts, but seldom do beliefs and actions change. The Spirit is mentioned, but people do not become spiritually vital. Small groups are formed, but community remains elusive.

The underlying problem with these churches is that they are in the business not of disciple making, but of church growing. Numbers, volunteers, and tithing amounts are used to judge growth and progress. Individuals can be expended as long as the mass of people, "the crowd," is returning and giving. More than anything else, people come away knowing more information, becoming more at home within the ethos of the church, and learning that church's praise songs by heart. Whether the church would admit it or not, it has become easier to do what has always been done than to question how we are helping people know Jesus personally and grow with him developmentally.

> We have found it easier to make churches that are exciting than to make disciples who are holy.

We have found it easier to make churches that are exciting than to make disciples who are holy. In turn, it takes so much energy to keep up a movement that upcoming leaders are rarely developed or mentored. It becomes necessary to hire people who are already "successful" elsewhere to do the same thing here. Ministry hiring soon looks little different than sports teams making a new acquisition or getting a first-round draft pick.

On a personal level, things are not much better. Clichés and self-help books offer short and easy steps to make life easier and happier, while the ideals of discipleship fall by the wayside. Life is too busy for things like daily community, so meeting with friends doubles as stress relief and much-needed human interaction; rarely do brothers and sisters in Christ shape and mentor each other. The busyness of the days makes interaction with God a chore and, more often than not, identities like mother, father, neighbor, jerk, boss are more foundational than those of Christian, child of God, disciple. All in all, at both the individual and the corporate level, within the solidified-minded context Christians are not developing a Christian way of seeing and interacting with reality.

If most churches and individuals are following this model, as I believe is the case, it is no wonder we have lost all ability to be a cultural presence.

A DEVELOPMENTAL JOURNEY

On the other hand, churches that follow a developmental model look much different. They accept in their very being that the Christian life is a journey of growth. This acceptance trains one's focus on God. The goal is to follow where he leads. In this setting, the whole point of Christian growth is the process. Such churches do not ignore any ideal about the Christian life, but they see it as a point on the horizon to journey toward, not a point in the past that we have already achieved that then permits us to just walk through life unchanged.

The church that accepts a developmental worldview is essentially relational, because the only way to change core beliefs—beliefs that inescapably rise to the surface of behavior and lifestyle, in private and everywhere else—is through relationships. Institutions as institutions can encourage people to accept propositions and even a general way of life, but they rarely change people's core beliefs. The assumption of many institutions is that core beliefs will somehow change miraculously, and therefore lifestyles will be miraculously renewed. Dallas Willard has said the church believes in "magic" sanctification, that if only we preach right, people will change. The belief that people change just by listening to a sermon could be one of the most detrimental naiveties in our church today.

A church on a developmental journey is on guard against this lack of change. While heresy is understood as a problem, the *metamorpha* model sees lack of change as a much greater problem. In order to combat this, *metamorpha* churches place a high priority on boundary, accountability, and support systems. They spurn pyramid-type structures where the top is the seat of all authority with no accountability.

> The belief that people change just by listening to a sermon could be one of the most detrimental naiveties in our church today.

This kind of church sees community as something to be learned. Just as most of my generation will get married with no firsthand knowledge of what a healthy marriage looks like, we will have to discover from scratch how to live in community, because all we know of community is being around other people who wonder what it looks like. In line with Scripture, the understanding of community is that we are to be known by the way we love one another, but we must also recognize that we cannot possibly do this without the Spirit working in the lives of individuals. Things like confession, evaluation, and depending on one another are daily practices, not because they are *normal* but because they are decidedly Christian. The church recognizes community as necessary for holiness, so an individual's spiritual life is a community issue. All believers know and understand their role in the body and see their task as disciples to be renewed according to what Scripture teaches us and how the Spirit guides.

The major difference between the *metamorpha* community and the stagnant one is that the former provides an environment in which it is possible to accomplish what the Bible commands. The "communion of saints" is no longer a nice cliché but an accomplished reality. The goals are certainly long-term, but they start with daily, hourly, and moment-by-moment discipleship. *Metamorpha* churches seek new believers intensely, but such churches will always help newcomers understand what it means to be involved in the community of God. This kind of church understands that it does not help the kingdom or non-Christians to have people in seats and only partially committed. At the same time, *metamorpha* recognizes perfection is impossible. Sin and failure are dealt with in love, recognizing that God works with his children in many different ways.

When *metamorpha* churches recognize bad fruit, two major things occur: First, the roots of the tree are addressed, in this case the Spirit, the Bible, and the community. The overriding assumption is that if the body is being renewed by God through the Bible while being empowered by the work of the Spirit within the context of community, good fruit will appear. Second, the church reassesses its programs because these are channels for the Spirit, the Bible, and community, and if a program ceases to be effective, it is either changed or dropped.

The point of the church is not to turn the means of ministering into ends in themselves but to be a functioning community that makes disciples; when that does not happen, the church needs to be re-formed. Good fruit comes from good trees, and so our job in addressing problems in the church (bad fruit) has to start with the roots (worldview informers) and then the programs (Sunday service, small groups, etc.). The end of these things should always be found in Jesus, and the informers and programs should continually point to him.

Leadership in this kind of church is plural, never individual. *Metamorpha* churches recognize that when individuals are in front, they tend to seek their own glory, not God's. Pastors follow Paul's example to go the extra mile in downplaying their importance, because they recognize that the highest goal is not information downloading, but life change. In this setting, the church is not preaching oriented, but mentoring oriented. It is not individually focused, but community focused. In this church, every member is an essential part of kingdom work; they are fellow workers and disciples whose jobs do not differ in importance from the pastor's but only take on different forms.

> *Metamorpha* sees individual sin as a corporate issue and deals with it as such, never in condemnation, but as part of the process of growth in the kingdom.

For the individual, the three major worldview informers are part of daily existence. *Metamorpha* keeps ideas like "the good life" and "being a Christian" in check by viewing them through the lenses of Spirit, community, and Bible. While the informers are not ends in and of themselves but gifts for righteousness, they are heeded as such and are used accordingly. Grace does not mean ignoring believers who are struggling; it means coming alongside them as they falter. *Metamorpha* sees individual sin as a corporate issue and deals with it as such, never in condemnation, but as part of the process of growth in the kingdom.

Believers on a developmental journey do not evaluate their relationship with God on the basis of time in study or acts of righteousness. Rather, they see every aspect of life within the context of God's presence. They take seriously the reality of the kingdom, both present and coming, when making daily decisions. In so doing they have their minds set on "things above" (Col. 3:2). Their "citizenship is in heaven" (Phil. 3:20), and they are living a life "worthy of the gospel of Christ" (Phil. 1:27).

The Christian life is not about arrival, but about learning to journey with God and becoming increasingly united with him.

Part 2

METAmorpha

A New Way of Being

4

THE WORD

Believer Deconstruction

After graduating from high school, I was confused, lost, and without any answers to the real questions in my heart. Going to a Christian college was a last-minute change of plans, and when the application asked for my major, I put down "Biblical Studies"—even though I knew nothing about the Bible.

I had never been given any tools for the Christian life when I was in high school. At the same time, I was never expected to be perfect, just to play the right role: go to the youth events, behave, and so forth. Shortly after I started college I came to realize I had no faith of my own, and I knew nothing of this God I supposedly "loved," whatever that meant. My solution to my emptiness was to learn all that I could about the Bible, thinking that if the solution was in those pages, then I would mine them to find it.[1]

I had always understood the Word as a sword in that it was a tool we could use, but I never expected the sword to turn back on me, piercing into the evil in my own heart.

Being honest with the Word uncovered a cavernous void in my heart. I had approached the Bible for so long without really relating to it that my faith and the faith talked about in the Bible were virtually incompatible. My solution to the problem was to do what I always did: stuff knowledge down my throat and hope that somehow my life would change—but that didn't work. The Bible moved me beyond what I knew and understood, and I felt my views of the world being undermined and deconstructed.

I came to see all I had believed and hoped for as being misguided and self-serving, and I realized all the things I had done to try to make God happy were really for my own glory. For the first time in my Christian life, I understood what the author of Hebrews meant when he said, "For the word of God is living and active and sharper than any two-edged sword, and piercing as far as the division of soul and spirit, of both joints and marrow, and able to judge the thoughts and intentions of the heart" (Heb. 4:12). My Christian experience was overwhelmed by a darkness I had not known before, and the darkness seemed to be inaugurated by the Word itself.

I had always understood the Word as a sword in that it was a tool we could use, but I never expected the sword to turn back on me, piercing into the evil in my own heart. I have recently discovered that many who walked the path before me discovered the same thing. In the words of Anthony Thiselton, "Luther and Calvin argued that the word of God encounters readers most sharply when it addresses us as adversary, to correct and change our prior wishes and expectations. . . . Grace and judgment, holiness and love, may recall us to new and better paths."[2]

It was during this darkness that I realized I had to make a choice. I could turn off my mind entirely and blindly accept everything that I had become comfortable with as someone who had grown up Christian and continue to read the Scriptures through that lens. This solution would at least allow me to once again feel better about myself. Or, in contrast, I could forge deeper into the painful unknown—only I didn't know what that meant. I knew I had to continue on the path where God led, somehow, but I had no idea what that meant either.

When I made the decision to continue with God, it was the first time I truly trusted him when it meant certain pain and frustration. I wasn't merely trusting him for something I couldn't control, like my salvation; I was asking to be led. When I went forward I entered with him into a world I didn't know—*his* world, where it made sense that his love required his son to die a ruthless death and that somehow last is first and first is last. I had always heard those things and "believed" them, but I had never expected them to mean anything in my life. But now I was the "poor in spirit," and while feeling totally defeated, I was the "blessed one."

During this time of my life, the Bible was a sharp sword that seemed to strike at me before I even opened it. I was tempted every time I touched it to stay in the Psalms, licking my perpetual wounds along with David for security. A moment came, however, when I was struck with the realization that I could either focus on a solution to my feeling of emptiness or I could actually trust that God can redeem. In a sense I was totally disenfranchised because of the Bible, completely separated and without a spiritual home, and yet it was through the Bible that I was shepherded into the flock by Jesus himself.

Unfortunately, it has become the norm to accept the Bible as nothing more than a database of information about God or, at best, an artist's palette with which we paint an image of him in our minds. This makes the Bible little different than a biography of, for example, Abraham Lincoln; we learn things about the person, but we fail to meet him in any real way. In order to interact with the Word in a more holistic way, we should engage it as history, shepherd, and friend.[3]

Just like the worldview informers, we all naturally gravitate toward one of these three ways of reading the Bible. The approach we take says a lot about our worldview, and limiting ourselves to that one way alone will limit the growth and formation that the Spirit wants to enact in our lives. This is why a discussion of how we read the Bible is so central to the task of belief formation.

It is important that we be aware of these three approaches as we read Scripture. In the second section of this chapter, we will look through the Gospel of Mark and examine it as one cohesive story Mark is telling about Jesus's way of belief formation. It was through wrestling with Mark's Jesus-epic that I came to see how important it is to interact with the Bible as history, shepherd, and friend. The deeper I got into the story, the more I heard from the historical Jesus. My ideas and concepts were deconstructed by him, and I felt like I was actually sitting at his feet, learning. I went from just reading about Jesus to listening to and relating with him.

History

In the midst of my confusion and disillusionment with Christianity, I did what many people do who feel totally inadequate about their relationship with God—I went to seminary. For many, seminary is as much a hospital as it is a training ground. For others, it is a way to push down what is really going on inside them while obtaining the highest level of evangelical devotion so they can be The Guy Who Knows the Bible.[4] To my surprise, seminary proved to be the place where God met me. I was warned by many that seminary would kill my relationship with God and burden my soul, and yet I found that it did quite the opposite.

One of my emphases in seminary was on the New Testament, including the world of the first century. For me, focusing on the ancient context of Scripture embodies what I mean by the term *history*. Scholars, both Christian and secular, have done an excellent job of using what we currently know about the first-century Jewish and Greco-Roman world to help us understand who Jesus was, what he was doing, and how his disciples functioned. As with any reading of the Bible, it is important to see Jesus in his context and realize that he was a real person with real followers who had similar tendencies as we do, even though they were in a different context.

A great example of this is N. T. Wright's book, *The Challenge of Jesus*, in which Wright approaches the Scripture as a historian and tries to show how someone in the first-century world would have seen Jesus, and possibly even how Jesus saw himself. As Wright has argued vigorously elsewhere, "We simply *can* write history. We can know things about what has happened in the past."[5] This history helps make Jesus and the Christianity we see in the Bible three-dimensional; it brings the text to life and helps people to understand more fully what is going on. We can know why Paul gets so angry at the Galatians, why Jesus starts flipping over tables in the temple, and why Jesus talks about remaining in the vine.

History has been, and must continue to be, the friend of every disciple who seeks to know and understand our Lord in deeper ways. But stopping here only gives us an incomplete view of the purpose of the text.[6]

SHEPHERD

My personal study of history brought me to understand this about Scripture: the Word is our shepherd. During seminary I came to a point where I no longer read the Bible merely for information but rather I opened myself to be led and guided by it. A well-developed understanding of history concerning the New Testament will automatically bring the reader to a place of choosing either to submit or to harden one's heart toward it in one way or another. The Word seeks to shepherd us—to guide us down a specific path from where we currently are.

In my quest for knowledge *about* God and the Bible, I was confronted by the realization that the texts I was studying were trying to move me. I was trying to learn about how ancient Christianity "worked," hoping that if I mimicked it in some way I would find the kind of life I was looking for, but the Bible wasn't interested in my agenda. As I see it now, the text was calling me to a new position of seeing. It was as if the Word was trying to help me peer around a corner in order to see past the very stumbling block that was hindering my ability to see in a kingdom way.

Some of the clearest examples of writing *for movement* are the parables. Parables have always made me think about my actions, my heart, and in what or whom I put my faith. As stated by Wright, parables "seem designed, within the worldview of the Jewish village population of the time, as tools to break open the prevailing worldview and replace

it with one that was closely related but significantly adjusted at every point."[7] These simple
yet subversive stories both tear down and
rebuild; they are the acts of deconstruction and reconstruction combined into
one.

> Jesus was not merely telling stories about some random, fictional reality; he was calling his hearers to *see the real world.*

Wright, in talking about Jesus's use
of parables, states, "Jesus was articu-
lating a *new way of understanding the
fulfilment of Israel's hope.* He had radi-
calized the tradition. This, as has often
been remarked in recent years, is how
stories work. They invite listeners into a
new world, and encourage them to make that
world their own, to see their ordinary world
from now on through this lens, within this grid. The
struggle to understand a parable is the struggle for a new
world to be born."[8] Jesus was not merely telling stories about
some random, fictional reality; he was calling his hearers to
see the real world.

What makes this even more interesting is the fact that
part of the nature of parables is actually to hide reality
(Matt. 13:13; Mark 4:11; Luke 8:10). K. R. Snodgrass states,
"Parables hide in order to reveal. Even though some would
respond with hardness of heart and lack of hearing, Jesus
taught in parables to elicit hearing and obedient response."[9]
Jesus appears to have spoken these parables to split crowds
down the middle; they reveal who is actually for him and
who is actually against him. In so doing, Jesus's ministry
forced an opinion about himself—people were either for him
or against him, but rarely were they without an opinion.

The Bible is constantly trying to guide us down paths
that we may not like but are for our benefit. When Paul

met Christ on the road to Damascus, Jesus said to him, "Saul, Saul, why are you persecuting Me? It is hard for you to kick against the goads" (Acts 26:14). Similarly, we often find ourselves kicking against the goads, as if God's Word is a cattle prod guiding us down paths of life. But to kick against them is to try to live according to our way instead of God's. We hurt ourselves instead of allowing the Word to move us. Certain texts are designed to guide us down another path than the one we are taking, to teach us what is really honorable or what "blessed" should actually look like, and to help us understand what Christian leadership looks like compared to that of the world. These texts help to refocus our vision in order to see the world in a way that is different from how we previously saw it.

As Scripture tried to shepherd me in the areas of my life where I was unbelieving and faithless, my first response was rarely (if ever) to turn to God but rather to change or ignore the text. More often than not, the temptation to focus on doctrine, grace, or another text would prevail, rather than coming to Jesus honestly about how little I even wanted to change—let alone how little I *had* changed (as if Jesus didn't know this himself). When the Spirit uses the text to open our hearts, we should proclaim, like David, "Search me, O God, and know my heart; try me and know my anxious thoughts; and see if there be any hurtful way in me, and lead me in the everlasting way" (Ps. 139:23–24).

Rarely do people ignore the text explicitly; instead, it becomes a habit of the heart to move on to a less painful subject, focus more on doctrine, or close up and just try harder. We fail to find peace in what the author of Hebrews tells us about the Word, "No creature is hidden from his sight, but all are naked and exposed to the eyes of him to whom we must give account" (Heb. 4:13 ESV). We can rest in the fact that we are laid bare, completely naked and honest before our Father in heaven. Our response then should be a journey with Christ through his Word, knowing that it is the sword that will tap into the depths of our being with hope, love, and discipline.

The Christian life is a journey, certainly, but not one of aimless wandering. It is a journey of increasing reliance upon the Shepherd. When life feels like aimless wandering, it is because you are being led through God's supernatural world but are trying to look at it through natural eyes that cannot see what, why, or how God is working. As our Shepherd, Jesus works in our hearts through the text, not merely through information, but through his Spirit by his Word.

> The Christian life is a journey, certainly, but not one of aimless wandering.

Our natural inclination will always be to push against the shepherding nature of Scripture. The second we "kick against the goad" of the Word, we undermine its deconstructing nature and make it into information alone. We act as a sheep that thinks he is above needing a shepherd and tries arrogantly to tell the shepherd where to go. Once we relativize Scripture around ourselves, it becomes nothing but information, and the temptation will always be to see it through our understanding of what the good life is, over against God's understanding of it. The text is an instrument to help us to see rightly, to take our eyes off the horizon at which they are aimed and align them with the horizon at which the text is really pointing, and this is only possible if we come to the text as sheep and continue on as sheep.[10]

As a holy text, we do not merely read the Bible—we relate with it. The Bible is an agent of the Triune God, whose purpose is to work in our hearts and minds and to allow for a true encounter with him through the text.[11] In relating with Scripture, we come to hear a God who has always been in the business of being with his people—and through the text, he speaks to our hearts.

The summer after my freshman year of college I was at a camp about an hour south of the Canadian border. There was no running water, no electricity, and I found myself spending a lot of time alone. For the first time in my life I had hours upon hours in each day to spend with God reading his Word—which I had never actually read before. I could understand what Anthony Thiselton meant when he said, "'Understanding' . . . is not simply scrutinizing a text as an 'object' of enquiry: it is more akin to listening to, and thereby coming to understand, a friend."[12] That summer, the text was the only friend I had.

I don't know if you have ever poured yourself into a book before, but because of my circumstances (alone, bored, nowhere to go), I actually poured the Bible into myself. I usually filled my time with friends, television, busyness, and noise, but now I had silence, solitude, and the Word. Eventually I began to feel as though, every time I came to it, I was sitting with an old friend I hadn't seen in years.

I had never really wanted to read the Bible before this time; it was foreign and weird, and I just didn't get it. Faced with an abundance of time, a lack of company, and nothing else to do but read, I sat for hours a day immersing myself in the text. Before long, I began to read, not for the sake of reading, but to relate to it, to know God through it. For the first time I realized how neutered my life had been up until that point; I had tried to walk a path I couldn't see because I was blind, without a guide, and refusing to ask for help.

Through my biblical immersion God took me on a tour of his world and showed me around. William Olhausen's thoughts sum up my experience: "What the Spirit speaks through the Word of scripture draws us into a public space with God himself; we can 'survey the world together.' In this way we begin to see how the Spirit draws the reader in to a new way of seeing the world that involves a crucial reorientation, and enabling, to *hear* scripture as God 'uses' it."[13] It was as if I had been trying to find God through ideas, while now God was by my side, walking with me.

Without knowing it, I was conversing with the Spirit of God about my life, about how I saw myself and how God sees me, and about the world around me and the way I interacted with it. Until that point, I only recognized the Spirit's work when something totally miraculous happened. The Bible told me I was more important than I thought I should be, and as a friend it came alongside me when no one else did.

If the Bible were just another book, it could still be a sword of sorts, but it could not be described as "living" and "active." This "sword of the Spirit" is a tool, not only for our battle with the demonic realm, but for our interaction with ourselves.[14] The Spirit is constantly at work in and through the text to guide, shape, and renew the mind and heart of the believer. It would be a tragedy if we only learned things *about* God, rather than *knowing* him and being shaped and developed by him.

In many ways, coming to the Bible as a friend is a lot like being on a first date. On a first date it is impossible to truly know one another; time is needed for that. So out of necessity, we use metaphors, analogies, and stories to talk about who we are, who we have been, and who we want to be. In the same way we come to the Bible and God tells us stories about who he has been and who he will be, he offers us metaphors of his character, and he uses analogies to describe his kingdom. It is only by spending time in real intimacy that we can actually come to know one another, just as in dating. Likewise, more and more of our life and the depths of ourselves are handed over to the other person as intimacy grows in depth, and through the Word and prayer we come to the same kind of intimacy with the Father.

I remember hearing about a man who was on trial in the Islamic world for becoming a Christian. This man, who refused to back down even when threatened with death, clung to his Bible during every proceeding. That picture has stuck with me. Here is a man who has been met by the Word, and he clings to it as a child would his mother. It is not that the Word has become his God but that it is the Word of the God who had sought him out and delivered him. He had found much more than words on a page, or facts about God, or arguments for God's existence; he was met by God himself. That is what we can have when we come to engage the Word fully, when we come to see it as much more than a book of facts about Jesus.

MARK'S EPIC OF BELIEVER DECONSTRUCTION

Since the Bible is the central tool used in believer formation and deconstruction, it is important to hear from the text itself to see how the Bible takes on this role. Mark's Gospel, as a whole, is written in such a way as to lead us through a process of worldview formation. As we see the major events of his story unfold, we can see how the history, shepherd, and friend aspects come into play in our devotional lives.

This has become, for me, one of the clearest and most relatable texts in the Bible. Mark gives us (two thousand years removed) a chance to become a member of the throng shadowing Jesus, seeking to follow him, and learning his ways. Like Jesus's disciples, we are to be surprised, admonished, and transformed.

In my study of the Gospel of Mark, I have come face-to-face with the idea of worldview deconstruction. In fact, after my study, I came to the conclusion that the book of Mark spells out the gospel of worldview deconstruction, and seeing it as such has proven to be a sharp sword for my soul. It is my hope that we can see Mark as a storyteller who wishes to take us into the world of the disciples and learn what it is to follow the man Jesus, even when we have no idea what that means.

> When it comes to really learning from the Bible, we run into a problem: believers tend to know "Jesus stories" a little too well.

When it comes to really learning from the Bible, we run into a problem: believers tend to know "Jesus stories" a little too well. We see the Gospels as storehouses for random anecdotes about Jesus, and we have heard them all a number of times, so we come to the Gospels with a "preglazed" mind-set. Coming to the Bible with an understanding of it as history, shepherd, and friend will ensure this does not happen; we can still be shocked, offended, and amazed about what Jesus is doing.

MARK'S BROAD STRUCTURE

To hear Mark's story correctly, it is important to walk through the elements of his narrative to see what he does and does not emphasize, how he tells his story, and what he lets us know about his purpose. Mark begins his tale in a way that is familiar to us but was obscure to his earliest readers: "The beginning of the gospel of Jesus Christ, the Son of God." Sadly, *we* hear two thousand years' worth of reflection when we read this, while the earliest readers would have heard something we do not, namely, "This is the beginning of the Good News about Jesus the King, the awaited Messiah." The word "Christ" merely means "king" or "anointed one," and the phrase "Son of God"[15] did not refer to the second member of the Trinity, because there was no belief in the Trinity before Jesus's ministry. At that time, the phrase "Son of God" meant "Messiah."[16]

We can see this clearly when Jesus calls Nathanael. Philip had already told Nathanael, "We have found Him of whom Moses in the Law and also the Prophets wrote—Jesus of Nazareth, the son of Joseph" (John 1:45), so he is expecting to find the Messiah or, in their terminology, the "Son of God." When Nathanael sees Jesus for the first time, he proclaims: "Rabbi, You are the Son of God; You are the King of Israel" (John 1:49). In his statement, his second phrase reemphasizes the first, *Jesus, you are the Messiah, the King.*

Unfortunately, we are so familiar with this language that it doesn't faze us. But how weird would it be to hear Nathanael, a good Jew, proclaim the Chalcedonian Creed out of nowhere: "Jesus, you are 'Truly God and truly man, of a reasonable soul and body; consubstantial with the Father according to the Godhead, and consubstantial with us according to the Manhood; in all things like unto us, without sin; begotten before all ages of the Father according to the Godhead.'"[17] Nathanael wasn't even thinking about a divine human; he was desperately seeking for the coming King, the Anointed One who would reign as Messiah.

Mark isn't trying to give us the Good News about Jesus as God, at least not yet, but about Jesus as the Messiah, which was the pressing concern for the Jewish worldview of the day. This is also why Mark includes John the Baptist, the one who was to prepare the way for Messiah, in his story. In our reading, it can be easy to see John as a "nice biblical figure," but in the ancient world, he was central to the teaching about the coming "Anointed One," the Messiah.

So to the ancient Jews, this was a weird way to begin a story. Starting by telling the readers about Jesus as Messiah seems like starting a joke by giving away the punch line; it would be like starting Cinderella with a side note: *Don't worry, she gets the prince in the end.* Many have assumed Mark was just a bad storyteller, but that is unlikely. Mark lived in an oral culture, a culture of storytelling. If any group has lost the ability to tell stories, we have, embedded as we are in a thoroughly visual culture. But Mark matches his odd beginning with an even worse ending—an ending so bad that people throughout time have either added a new one or have argued that we must have lost Mark's original. (Just look in your translation—everything past 16:8 is added.)

So just what is this supposedly lousy ending? After the resurrection of Jesus, the young man at the tomb tells the woman to go and tell the disciples and Peter about what has happened, and Mark ends the "Good News" like this: "They went out and fled from the tomb, for trembling and astonishment had gripped them; and they said nothing to anyone, for they were afraid." This hardly reads like the good news Mark set us up for in his introduction. In fact, if anything, it would seem that the good news has gone awry. But the fact that Mark insists this is good news should clue us in to the fact that we must be missing a central element to the story. Somewhere there must be a twist that will help all this make sense—and as we will see below, that is exactly what Mark gives us.

It is relatively easy to see how Mark's story informs us historically, since it is technically a historical narrative. The striking aspect of Mark's Gospel is that he is telling us about the Messiah—a topic every Jew in the ancient world would want to know about. In this sense, he is offering the text as shepherd. Mark writes to inform and change your opinion as to who the Messiah is, and through his text we can even come to relate with this Messiah. Mark's Gospel is shocking from beginning to end in its approach to the question that first-century Jews were asking: "Who is this Jesus, and should I get to know him?"

> The striking aspect of Mark's Gospel is that he is telling us about the Messiah—a topic every Jew in the ancient world would want to know about.

MARK'S STYLE

Mark isn't just a regular storyteller; he is the "guy in the bar with a little too much information" kind of a story-teller. Mark's literary style has frequently been described as "barbarous" or "unrefined."[18] His Gospel moves incredibly fast (he uses the word *immediately* forty-two times), but he uses significantly more words and detail in his stories than the same stories in Matthew or Luke.[19] This makes Mark's Gospel more lifelike, pulling the reader into the narrative. At one point Mark tells us about Jesus, who is "looking about at those who were sitting around Him" (Mark 3:34); it is through his language that we get to sit there as well, with Jesus teaching *us* specifically.

Mark skips a year of Jesus's ministry entirely, from the point of his time in the desert to Jesus calling disciples to himself. He certainly knows about those years, but they don't fit into his overall purpose for writing. There are also no genealogies or birth narrative. Mark drops us into the story at the point where Jesus starts putting together his group of kingdom leadership.

> Mark isn't just a regular storyteller; he is the "guy in the bar with a little too much information" kind of a storyteller.

Mark clearly tries to shepherd the reader somewhere, which is emphasized by his constant geographical movement between stories: each story begins with a journey or movement of some kind. The Gospel as a whole mimics this, tracing Jesus's quest from Galilee to Jerusalem, the city that is seeking out her Messiah. The story is like following a presidential nominee all the way from his hometown to the White House; Mark follows Jesus on his way to the throne in Jerusalem.

Mark refrains from using large blocks of narrative where Jesus just preaches and instead shows Jesus during his encounters with people (scribes, Pharisees, disciples, and others). This shows Jesus interacting with various worldviews of the day and lets the reader see Jesus in different contexts. In using this method, Mark allows us to walk around with Jesus, soften or harden our hearts, and see which group we follow most naturally. As we relate with Jesus, we also will relate with those who follow him, those who reject him, and those who are ambivalent.

So what kind of story is Mark telling? As Mark himself admits, it is the story of the Good News of the Son of God. The reader of Mark's Gospel quickly comes to see, if nothing else, that no one has any idea who Jesus really is, including his disciples. He is called teacher, prophet, Son of Man, Son of David, and more, and yet no one seems to understand why he is behaving the way he is. Mark tells a story that has many contrasts, but the most pervasive seems to be "the way of God" versus "the way of man."[20] These are opposing ways of seeing reality: one finds its source in God; the other finds its source in man. Mark calls us to choose which one we will follow.

Because Mark is telling a story about the coming King, his story answers the questions that every Messiah-seeking Jew was asking. We don't have too many stories like this anymore. It would be the equivalent of a story today that answers questions like: What is the meaning of life? Where will the next terrorist bombing be? What happens when I die? Mark proposes to answer the question that plagued every Jew's mind, and with his style, he pulls the reader/hearer into a group of Jewish boys following this would-be Messiah on his conquest of Jerusalem, the place where the Messiah would reign.

Because Mark's audience desperately wanted to know the outcome of this Good News, they already had the story played out in their minds. As we've already discussed, one of the major aspects of worldview is that it offers a way that things should be and is used to make decisions based on what one believes will be true. The Jewish people had a story already established in their minds about what the Messiah was going to do, and Mark brings the reader into a relationship with a Messiah who has a different story to tell.

CONFLICT IN MARK'S STORY

When this Gospel is seen as a whole, there is a distinct center to the narrative.[21] To understand the story Mark tells, it is essential to take the beginning, the middle (the major conflict), and the end into account instead of breaking the story down and focusing only on one segment at a time. In ancient times this story would have been read aloud and all at once, so these things would have been evident to the ancient hearers. We do an injustice to the historical and shepherding aspects of the text by ignoring these larger plotlines.

> Mark brings the reader into a relationship with a Messiah who has a different story to tell.

As Mark weaves together the first half of his Good News, one thing becomes clear: Jesus is an unusual king. He keeps telling people not to talk about him, he often removes himself from crowds, and he refers to himself as the Son of Man—which is just another way to say "man" or to refer to oneself.[22] To those expecting to hear the story of the campaigning king, Jesus was acting weird, being elusive, and speaking of himself in an ambiguous way.

The conflict in the story is both the high point and the low point in the Gospel thus far. Jesus asks his disciples, "Who do people say that I am?" which is an important worldview question. Jesus has been ambiguously referring to himself as the Son of Man, and yet they were not looking for the Son of Man; they were looking for the Messiah, the Son of God. When the disciples answer, they reveal the present gossip about Jesus: some say "John the Baptist, and others say Elijah, but others, one of the prophets." Clearly Jesus doesn't fit in any preconceived categories people had. Then Jesus asks who the disciples think he is, and Peter blurts out, "You are the Christ" (Mark 8:27–29).

This response is monumental because Jesus has finally gotten the disciples to the place where he wants them—they finally understand. After telling them not to tell anyone that he is the Christ, Jesus begins teaching them that he has to suffer; this is the first time in the Gospel that Jesus links suffering with being the Messiah.[23] Peter gets up, probably still glowing from his previous interaction with Jesus, and rebukes him. This, in miniature, is the Gospel of Mark as a whole. To Peter, and no doubt to the rest of the disciples, Jesus is the Messiah, which means he is going to restore the kingdom of Israel and become king. But that also means that they can't understand why Jesus needs to suffer and die, and so Peter hears a mouthful from Jesus about not thinking the things of God, but of men.

The Gospel of Mark is, in this way, an account of worldview deconstruction about the Messiah. The purpose of this book is to shepherd the reader: it seeks to change what you believe about the Jesus of history and what kind of king he was. All the other themes (geographical, paradoxical, suffering, etc.) revolve around this one. It is the Gospel that forces the reader to surrender his or her own categories of who Jesus should be and offers a deeper, mysterious, and otherworldly Messiah for acceptance.

Mark sets up his story so that the structure points out the disciples and their conflict with Jesus (over against the conflict with the Jewish leadership), showing how even the ones closest to Jesus struggle to get beyond their own worldview. Peter, as the representative of the disciples, serves as the poster child for worldview deconstruction. According to tradition, Mark's Gospel is derived from the preaching of Peter himself, so we can see how Peter uses his own story to show what can happen when one's worldview is arrogant. Peter uses his own shortcomings to help guide others to avoid the mistakes he made.

Mark's Twist

The twist in Mark's story stems from the voice of Jesus himself. Jesus constantly refers to himself as the "Son of Man" —a phrase that did not have any significant meaning for people.[24] I believe he did so specifically because it had no meaning; therefore, Jesus could fill it with the meaning he wanted: suffering servant, Messiah, King, and more. Jesus knows that once he lets on that he is the Messiah, people will try to force him to fit into their messianic box—something that actually did happen (John 6:15). Even the questioning Jesus receives from the high priest is about whether or not he is "the Christ, the Son of the Blessed One" (Mark 14:61).

Jesus's response to the high priest is revealing: he states that he is in fact the Christ, and that they will see "the Son of Man sitting at the right hand of Power" (Mark 14:62). Suddenly, Jesus fills the phrase "Son of Man" with meaning; by quoting a passage from Daniel 7, he aligns himself with God. *This was Jesus's blasphemy.* This is the reason he was crucified. The major twist in the story is that the Jewish Messiah came as the Son of Man, and his own people did not recognize him. As an ancient hearer of the story, you would think back to all of the times Jesus referred to himself as the

"Son of Man," and suddenly it would be clear that Jesus saw his ministry as much more than a political campaign. You would finally see that God had once again heard the cries of his people, and this time, he had come personally to do something about it.

The major twist in the story is that the Jewish Messiah came as the Son of Man, and his own people did not recognize him.

At the end of the Gospel, Jesus's followers disperse, their worldviews unable to accommodate what is happening. The last person in Mark's story to call Jesus the Son of God is a Roman centurion, someone whose worldview doesn't have the same presuppositions as the Jewish one. It is Jesus's death that helps him to see who Jesus really is. Suffering, a major theme in Mark, is a stumbling block for those with a solidified worldview about the Messiah, and it is the light of God for those whose worldview remains pliable.

Since Mark is trying to demonstrate how Jesus's worldview is entirely opposite of the world's, he shows many different groups confused, frustrated, and even scared because of what Jesus says and does. It is not surprising, then, that Mark ends the Gospel with some of Jesus's closest companions living in fear and not telling anyone about this Good News. Many think this ending is incomplete and refuse to believe Mark would close his story this way. However, this is a great ending by a great storyteller whose story revolves around a King who refuses to be the people's Messiah so he could be God's.

MARK'S PURPOSE

Mark does not write his story the way we would because we are better journalists than storytellers. We think in terms of "give me the facts and only the facts," while Mark tries to tell a story that will subvert the reader's view of the world. Mark's purpose is not to write down everything he knows about Jesus; that wouldn't accomplish what he desires. His purpose is to show how Jesus either turned people away from himself or brought people to him to have their views of Israel, God, and the world turned upside down—and Mark's call is the same to us today.

It is especially important to note what Mark says he is doing at the very beginning of his story: he is writing the *beginning* of the Good News.[25] Mark ends his story the way he does because his story talks about the *real* world. People could then stop reading about this upside-down Messiah and look around them to see upside-down disciples being killed for their faith. Mark doesn't have to redeem the disciples in his story because Jesus redeemed them in real life, and now they are turning the world on its head. The story ends where our reality begins, and we are to go out and live according to the ways of God and not the ways of man. Mark's story is a preface to the story we tell the world today.

It is easy to see the historical and shepherding implications of Mark's story; they are around every corner. And the relational facet of the text shines through as we are drawn into the story and given the chance to meet with Jesus, hear from him, and actually see him looking at us as we sit with the other disciples. We are allowed to respond to the calls of Jesus like his disciples, like the crowds following, or like the scribes and Pharisees.[26] The Spirit has something to say to us in the text, and we must relate to it honestly and openly as the Spirit goes to work on our hearts.

Just as in the Bible as a whole, Mark allows us to meet with Jesus and, in our seeking, find God. The text exists, in part, to deconstruct the believer and the seeker and to further

> We all eventually come to the place where we must admit we do not understand the words of Christ and do not want to follow them, but, like Peter, we must recognize that they are in fact words of eternal life.

harden those who harden their hearts against the way God calls his people to see the world. Although we have been using "belief deconstruction" as our phrase for this process, it may be more accurate to talk about "belief liberation." God's molding will often feel more negative, like deconstruction, but if we take Jesus at his word, he is using all things as ways to liberate us from our present struggles and bring us into the reality of his love. As put by John Coe:

> The basic means by which God by his Spirit conveys his presence for Christian formation is through the revelation of his truth, or his Word. This divine truth becomes dynamic in the process of transformation by the presence of the Spirit who teaches and applies it to the human heart (cf. Jer. 31:33–34; Isa. 54:13; 1 Cor. 2:9–13). . . . Transformation comes through the appropriation of God's truth in the word into the depths of our heart so that his truth is incorporated into our being and controls our behavior.[27]

After hearing some of his teaching, most of the disciples leave Jesus, saying, "This is a difficult statement, who can listen to it?" When Jesus asks Peter if he will leave as well, Peter responds by saying, "Lord, to whom shall we go? You have words of eternal life" (John 6:60, 66–68). Peter does not understand Jesus any more than the other disciples do, but he chooses to follow and allows Jesus's words to form how he sees the world.

We all eventually come to the place where we must admit we do not understand the words of Christ and do not want to follow them, but, like Peter, we must recognize that they are in fact words of eternal life. Our believing Christ's claims does not depend on our agreement or understanding but upon following and trusting that God's way of seeing reality is more informed than our own.

At the end of Mark, in all our Bibles, we have an extra paragraph that was added after Mark wrote the Gospel. At the end of a story that focuses on seeing the world God's way instead of our way, we have tacked on a new ending because we didn't understand. Do you see the irony? I am reminded of what was once said to me by a popular young evangelical pastor concerning a question of doctrine: "I didn't like what the Bible said . . . so I changed my view of the Bible." Sometimes our presuppositions and assumptions are no different than adding to or removing from the Bible itself, and sometimes we'll go so far as to change our view of the Bible so it will say what we want it to say. It will only be by the grace of God and the work of his Spirit that we will one day be able to look past our arrogant views of the world and learn to submit to what we do not understand.

5

THE SPIRIT

The Breath of Life

Reading the Bible anew brought so much of my Christian understanding into question that it shocked me. One of the most significant areas of deconstruction was my understanding of the Holy Spirit. One of the most radical messages of any religion is the idea that the Spirit of God has come to dwell within his people. But this was not the message I heard when Christianity was explained to me, nor was it the explanation of the Christian life I received. I was offered a view of living with Christ without the reality of that intimacy—the Spirit of God in my heart.

My Christian life failed to be "spiritual" because I was the one who was trying to activate change.[1] I made the gospel a law for entering the kingdom, and I thought I had to work hard to be accepted. I came to Christianity on my terms, believing I would be the one controlling my development. Yet, as I came to learn, the Spirit is the agent of change in our lives, and because we often fail to relate to and interact with him as such, change remains elusive. We may have to work hard—change does not come by itself—but that hard work is similar to the work we do in a marriage or a friendship rather than that of career development.

That the role of the Spirit has been the missing element of Christian doctrine, devotion, and practice is evident as far back as 1897, when Pope Leo XIII said the following:

> We should direct towards Him [Holy Spirit] the highest homage of our love and devotion. Christians may do this most effectually if they will daily strive to know Him, to love Him, and to implore Him more earnestly. . . . All preachers and those having care of souls should remember that it is their duty to instruct their people more diligently and more fully about the Holy Ghost . . . so that errors and ignorance concerning matters of such moment may be entirely dispelled, as unworthy of "the children of light."[2]

Part of the Good News that we call the gospel is that we do not naturally become holy, but we do so supernaturally—through the Spirit within us. I used to see faith as a leap into darkness, but now I understand it to be a leap into a world I know to be true because of the work of the Spirit in my life. Growing in faith is growing in our ability to *see rightly*, and we are powerless to do that outside of the Spirit.

I don't want to focus here on whether or not the Spirit still works in miraculous ways or even on how the Spirit behaves. And while it's tempting to talk about the Spirit in terms of the other two worldview informers, because he empowers them both, I want to avoid that as well. Instead, my focus here will be on what we must understand about the person of the Spirit to help us hand over our worldviews for transformation. To help us with this, I will discuss the Spirit in terms of transforming relationally, formational intimacy, and life from within.

Transforming Relationally

Like most of the Christians in my generation, I have a history of floating around to various churches to sample the "good preaching" (which is slang for exciting, charismatic, interesting, and often novel) and "good worship" (which is slang for good music, good environment, and the "right" feel, which is also everything we look for in a good bar). But a time came when I realized that many of my heroes in the church were either morally questionable or "formationally challenged," and after this realization I stopped going to church for a long time because I was disillusioned and frustrated.

After several years of popping in and out of churches and reevaluating what all of this "Christian" stuff was about, I discovered certain questions I had never bothered asking, and what no one had ever bothered asking me. I had followed excitement, information, rhetoric, charisma, and all the programs churches had to offer, but I had never heard about a leader's relationship with the Holy Spirit, nor had anyone ever asked about mine. I sat in countless accountability groups with unending clichés, doctrine, and confession of sin, but I never knew how much my fellow brothers prayed or whether or not all of this excitement was going anywhere.

As theologian R. A. Torrey stated long ago, "A frequent source of error and fanaticism about the work of the Holy Spirit is the attempt to study and understand His work without first of all coming to know Him as a person."[3] We often talk about the Spirit in light of his fruit or power, but rarely do we really know the Spirit as the person who lives within us.

> It is essential for worldview transformation that we know the Spirit as a person.

This is why understanding and being influenced by the three worldview informers is so important. When we as a body of believers take the life of *metamorpha* seriously, we can stop the incessant, pendulumlike swinging of the church and finally find a balance where we can focus our attention on Christ and be a people of the Spirit. We can then walk a path of liberation from our own ideals and desires and open up to the kingdom reality. We can put aside our understanding of power and rest in the God whose desire is to be with people.

It is essential for worldview transformation that we know the Spirit as a person. One pastor, after coming to see the importance of a relationship with the Spirit, says this:

> I believe it is safe to say that no matter how much you know the Bible, no matter how much you discipline yourself, no matter how hard you try to serve and please God, if you are not properly related to the Spirit of God, the Christian life will not work for you. That's because the Christian life is not a ritual or a set of teachings but a relationship—a relationship with God through His Holy Spirit.[4]

We do not change because of a "force," from memorizing doctrine, or by acting out the externals of the Christian life; we change when we learn to relate in love with the God *who is love*. In relegating the Spirit's work exclusively to what we have experienced and understand, the Spirit ceases to be a person to relate with and becomes instead a "thing" to be categorized, tapped into, manipulated, or ignored. In any case, we have, in the words of Stanley Burgess, "shown more concern for the gifts than for the Giver."[5]

It would be tragic if we spent our lives trying to *do* Christianity, when it is clear that it cannot be done on our own. Only the Spirit knows our hearts, our sins, and the answer to our frustrations, and it is only in relating to him and coming to know him as the person who lives within us that we can truly learn to walk with God. We learn to journey well when we come to see that the path we tread is not a lonely one, but one with the God who knows the way.

THE QUIET SOURCE OF STRENGTH

When I tried to pray for long periods of time, I became extremely frustrated. I would usually start out excited to come to the Spirit in search of guidance and direction and finish the prayer feeling tired, ignored, and confused. After one such time, I remember thinking that I had spent an hour in silence with God and nothing was accomplished because of it. In that moment, the Spirit spoke.

I did not hear an audible voice, but the Spirit seemed to grab my head and focus my sight in the right direction. I immediately realized that the time I spent focusing on God had nothing to do with him and had everything to do with what I could possibly receive in that time. The "relationship," if it could be called that, existed to serve me; and God, with his infinite patience, slowly fixed my sight on the reality that my vision was fixed firmly on my own desires.

The more I evaluate my feelings about the Christian life, the more I realize what I really believe. I now know that I only wanted to use the Spirit for power, blessing, and success and had never really considered coming to know the Spirit intimately. It was the spiritual version of wanting marriage for sex, joy, and happiness but not love, intimacy, and growth. But as I have learned, the Spirit doesn't want to be used; he wants to be known. A relationship with the Spirit is like a relationship with anyone else: we want to be loved for who we are, not for what we bring to the table. We know this to be true in every relationship we have ever had, and that doesn't change just because it's God to whom we are now relating.

Over time it became clear that I didn't find it satisfying enough to just *be* with God.[6] I could sit in the presence of the almighty God, who was living within me, and yet I would leave feeling like nothing occurred. I wanted answers, words, action, or at least some warm feelings, and yet it seemed to be more important to God that I sit and wait.

Waiting has never really made sense to me. The Western church raised me to think about action, to think about Christianity as a verb. The Spirit seems to be less interested in these things than I am. This started making sense once I was able to put my view aside and allow the Spirit to show me the ways of God.

The Spirit is a lot like the weather. The weather changes at will, beyond anything we can control. Our role is to respond to the weather accordingly, to understand what it is doing before we decide what we will do. Yet we are often the ones trudging through snow in flip-flops because we want God (and the weather) on our terms instead of adjusting our life to his mission and will. This may mean that we live our Christian life exactly like our parents did, or it can mean that we have relegated spirituality to things we do on a Sunday morning. Whatever the case, we tend to be a people who want the Spirit to come alongside of what we are doing and tend to avoid seeking the Spirit's will over our own.

I went through a two-year experience where I felt totally abandoned by God— yet God did more in my life during that time than in all of the times combined when I felt him near. This taught me that God's closeness has nothing to do with my feelings and that everything I did to try and control, evaluate, and measure God's presence was out of my own self-centeredness, pride, and arrogance. The Spirit will work within our hearts, in our context, in very specific ways, and yet we often fight against him. It may be that we have no room in our worldview for God to work; we come to God expecting an experience, when God is in the business of making people holy (1 Thess. 4:3–8).

> We come to God expecting an experience, when God is in the business of making people holy.

The Spirit has much to show us, but we often come to him caring much more about speaking rather than listening, about doing rather than becoming, and about our desires rather than finding his. For many, this may mean learning about God rather than serving him or, for others, doing Christian deeds instead of growing in intimacy (through prayer, meditation, etc.). There isn't any kind of relationship where this behavior would be appropriate, and yet that is often how I have tried to relate with God. We can talk about being missional, relevant, and reaching the world, but it is all pretend unless we are trees planted by the living waters and are bearing those things as fruit.

As I sat down to write this chapter, my first inclination was to write one sentence and leave it at that: "The Holy

Spirit is the Triune Creator God living within our hearts, personally ministering to our souls, and we will never be certain what he is doing, how he is praying, or where he is leading until we submit humbly to the fact that he is God and we are not." That was going to be the whole chapter. I found myself thinking, as was said by the fourth-century writer Hilary of Poitiers, "I cannot describe Him whose pleas for me I cannot describe."[7] End of story. End of discussion.

But in the end I decided that there *is* more to be said, albeit not much more. In my take on worldview development, it is essential that we understand that the Spirit will do as he wills, and our role is to relate with him. Our faith "has legs" when we start trusting the Spirit for our growth and for a new way of seeing the world and everything in it. Our temptation will be to allow programs and schemes to clutter the silence necessary for hearing the God who resides within us. My hope is to sweep aside all that may be clouding the issues of the Spirit so we may open up to the transforming work the Spirit can do.

Formational Intimacy

I remember hearing a message many years ago by Rob Bell, founding pastor of Mars Hill Bible Church in Grandville, Michigan. He focused on the fact that our God has always been, and continues to be, the God who wants to come down and hang out with his people. Until that time, somewhere in my mind I had separated Jesus, the Spirit, and the Father so much that I had forgotten that the God who pitched a tent among his people has now actually made me into his own personal tent as well. Few have made this come alive as well as Carlo Carretto:

I am a dwelling place. I am not alone. In the secret depths of my poor human substance is the presence of God. Not a God who is solitary, but a God who is Trinity, a God who is love. A God who is Father, a God who is Son, a God who is Holy Spirit. But a God made One by love. And a God whose love enables me to become one with Him. . . . I believe that no moment exists for man which is more important, more beautiful, more dramatic, more decisive, more radical, than the moment when he becomes aware of—or rather, "lives"—this reality.[8]

Jesus offered conversion to a way of life, and the Jesus way of life is the enacted parable of the Spirit. In Jesus's life, we find the contrasts and contradictions that make parables so informative: Jesus is king, and yet he is a poor carpenter's son; he is God, and yet he has emptied himself of everything; he has power over all, and yet he is killed by mere men. Jesus, like the parables, breaks down worldviews by coming into contact with them.

Unfortunately, when we focus so intently on Jesus as God, we can neglect that he is the perfect example of man. Nothing would have been more obvious to the disciples than the simple reality that Jesus was fully human. It wouldn't have even occurred to them to think otherwise.[9] On the other hand, understanding Jesus as God would have been extremely difficult. It could be that the reason so many of us have struggled through the Christian life is that we have lost all possibility for Jesus to be an example of how to live because we see him first as God and only second (if at all) as human.

Jesus's life, to the people around him, was not the kind of life God would live if he were to walk among his people. Of course the idea that God would walk among them as a man would never have entered their minds! The life of Jesus was the kind of life a man would live when he was filled with the Spirit of God. I'm not referring to specific events but to *the way* Jesus lived his life. Jesus was a "good tree" because he was intimately connected with the Spirit. Because his life was led by the Spirit, he was able to live according to a spiritual reality, but this was not because he was God. All the miracles Jesus did, all the acts of power and the life of mercy and grace that he lived were possible because he was a man with the Spirit, not because he was God.[10]

> The tragedy of our age is that we tend not to think of ourselves as those who have the Spirit within them; instead we label ourselves by the things we can *do* by the power of the Spirit.

Failing to see Jesus as anything less than the perfect example of abundant life is a failure to allow the parable of Jesus to penetrate our hearts. Jesus acted, lived, healed, preached, and everything else out of the power of the God with whom he related in his inner being. In speaking about the counselor to come (John 16:7), Jesus said that it would be to the advantage of the disciples that Jesus left so that the Spirit would be with them. We are now empowered to live the kind of life Jesus did, to function in the kingdom of God as Spirit-people. We are called to walk in the way that Jesus walked, not on the same path, but from the same source—the indwelling Spirit of God.

It can be easy in the busyness of our world today to ignore that the Spirit of the living God is actually living within us. The tragedy of our age is that we tend not to think of ourselves as those who have the Spirit within them; instead we label ourselves by the things we can *do* by the power of the Spirit.

We often give a higher status to those who are used by the Spirit for teaching, writing, foreign missions, and so forth, because we tend to categorize gifts by their supposed quality as opposed to their function. The easy solution for this would be to just try and mimic kingdom values and actions, to do the work of the Spirit on our own. But the kingdom of God is about people functioning *from* a relationship with God; our role is to grow with the Spirit from the depths of our being, and not merely in what we do.[11] Higher status in the kingdom, therefore, has nothing to do with function and everything to do with relationship. The difference is between a person vying for power and authority, getting education and impressive contacts, and running for political office to advance his or her "reign," and Mother Teresa, who avoided the limelight, avoided politics and networking, and yet was one of the most powerful figures of her generation—someone who trumped anyone's power and authority. Hers was the power of the kingdom, one that stemmed from a relationship with the one who has the power rather than through her trying to function in a powerful way.

It is in our intimate relationship with the Triune God that we come to see ourselves, him, and our mission in God's terms and no longer our own. Mother Teresa didn't become a powerful figure by putting herself in a position of authority but by positioning herself in a relationship with God. It is only after we have come to understand that without God we can do nothing that our minds are drawn above—where Christ is seated at the right hand of God (Col. 3:1–2)—and when we can live in this world according to that reality.

It is through this formational intimacy with the Spirit that we are guided along a path of growth. While this process may be continual, it rarely feels as though we are growing continually. As Burgess has beautifully put it, "Yet the action of the Holy Spirit in our souls is so quiet and so continuous that it is barely perceived. He who breaks into our lives, unbounded by natural restraints, is a Person gentle. Yet He is God active within us."[12] It is this "quiet" and "continuous" work that we often fail to acknowledge as the Spirit's doing. Yet it is this God who comes to live and relate to us in our very hearts. One theologian has said: "The real theme of the doctrine of the Holy Spirit is that of human life and growth in relation to God, for by the power of the Spirit we are drawn into the fellowship of the Father and the Son. This, however, stands in sharp conflict with the central concerns of modern Western thought and culture, where the autonomy of human beings, their self-fulfilling potentiality and freedom, has become the normative concern."[13]

This "central concern of modern Western thought and culture" is a window into our worldview. When the Spirit is seen through a Western worldview, he often becomes an empowering force rather than an intimate friend. Failing to see our relationship with the Spirit in relational terms (marriage, union, intimacy) will typically lead to an impersonal focus on ourselves rather than God.

Jesus promises the good life, but it will never be the good life we have envisioned for ourselves, no matter how holy we think our intentions are. We just happen to have a God who is much more creative than we are, and trusting him means, in the very least, resting in his infinite imagination.

Our journey will probably have to look much like the psalmists', who often cried out to God with utmost honesty about their inability to find him near. Our honesty will be the place where God teaches us humility, trust, and how to really be loved. I have found in my own life that the Spirit longs for me to come to him as I honestly am, with what is really going on inside me and how I actually see the world. When I do, he takes me and shows me how little I understand and how much he has to teach me.

Because of the nature of intimacy with the Spirit, it is most often in prayer that we come to have this intimate relationship with God. James Houston states, "Encountering God in prayer is not always comfortable. Prayer exposes us to the character of God, who comes up against our own sinfulness. God's character collides with the sinful character of the culture in which we live and which deeply infects us as people."[14] Our prayers have to be more than lists of things we want God to be aware of; we have to come to meet God in our prayers.

Our prayers have to be more than lists of things we want God to be aware of; we have to come to meet God in our prayers.

I am reminded of how I saw marriage back in my single days. I constantly thought about the wedding being the door to walk through, where struggle and work would finally end. But from this side of things, I know that the wedding was the starting line for an incredible journey with my wife of learning, growing, and wrestling through the painful realities of our brokenness. Along with that, I realize now that entering into marriage is a journey in worldview development.

Kelli, my wife, will continue to help me see reality in a new way and will continually speak spiritual truths into my life through the work the Spirit is doing inside her. As you can probably see, the Christian life is no different. As said by Clark Pinnock, "Being saved is more like falling in love with God."[15] It is in this love with God that he helps us to see the world, ourselves, and, as we have seen in Mark's Gospel, even God himself in deeper and deeper ways. As in marriage, our journey with God is a journey into reality—one that demands our honesty, faith, and belief that the journey is the whole point.

In marriage we become one flesh with one another, while in conversion we become one Spirit with Christ (1 Cor. 6:17). The journey begins as a quest to know our spouse intimately, and as we learn more, our vision of that relationship will continue to adapt and grow. If it does not, stagnancy in marriage, as in Christianity, is what leads many down a path of less and less intimacy and even relational death.

LIFE FROM WITHIN

In John 7:37–38 Jesus proclaims, "If anyone is thirsty, let him come to Me and drink. He who believes in Me, as the Scripture said, 'From his innermost being will flow rivers of living water.'" Likewise, Paul states that the Spirit searches our hearts and prays for us (Rom. 8:26–27). After living within Christian circles for a while, we can become so familiar with these passages that we fail to hear how revolutionary their messages are. The mistake is to make these into statements for us to affirm without ever really thinking about what they mean.

The understanding that the Triune God *is within us* has to be more than an intellectual assent, as if we can just sign off on a doctrinal statement and be filled with the reality of God. As Colin Gunton noted, "The Trinity has more often been presented as a dogma to be believed rather than as the living focus of life and thought."[16] The concept of the Trinity is not something we can just tack onto a set of beliefs we already have, but it is a reality that changes everything—we cannot see the world as we once did. It would be like a blind man seeing for the first time. His sight would not be the only thing affected, but the way he related to, thought about, and interacted with the world would be totally revolutionized.

We have within us the source of all life—guiding, sustaining, and leading us down paths of righteousness. There is no amount of words that can explain what this looks like, nor can it be explained to those who haven't experienced it. It is like asking a person what it is like to be in love when you have never experienced it for yourself.

Fortunately, there are several things we *can* know that are clear about the Spirit as the indwelling spring of life within us. We know that just because someone has the Spirit does not mean that they see the world in a spiritual way (1 Cor. 3:1). We know that the Spirit can be foiled by our worldviews, and we can go on living according to our own nature and desires, never handing over to God our view of the world in exchange for his. We know this because we see this kind of thing happen all the time, either in our own lives or in the lives of others.

Of all the relationships I have had, my relationship with the Spirit has been the most elusive and yet the most dependable. The feelings of peace, elation, emptiness, and joy that he can bring are on his agenda alone, and nothing can predict it. I can remember one such emotion that came in college when I was walking through campus. My college's campus was a small but picturesque one in the Midwest. There was a stream running through the middle (right behind my dorm), and the entire area was wooded. This particular night was warm for the winter, a blistering thirty degrees (which when you live there actually does feel warm). I was walking across campus coatless and was amazed at how sharp the night sky was.

> We have within us the source of all life—guiding, sustaining, and leading us down paths of righteousness.

In that moment, God revealed something in my own heart that was so funny I laughed out loud. I know I must have looked crazy, and I hope that no one saw me. I never bothered writing down what God revealed to me in that moment; I was certain it would be impossible to forget. Of course you know what that means: I forgot it. For a while, this really bothered me, but I think it was more important for me to realize that God is near, regardless of where I am. God wasn't offering me information but intimacy.

It was in the moment that I realized God cared enough about me to be with me, draw close to me, and reveal himself to me that I truly found joy in being with God. My joy up to that point had been found in the effects of God—my own peace, my own ministries within his body, and the like. But this was very different. I was able to laugh with God, and I was overcome with his presence and his fellowship.

I also remember God's presence being nearly debilitating; his holiness was too much for me to handle, and my own lack of worth was too great for me to bear. I remember feeling exposed and naked, shameful and depressed. Looking to God in that moment did not bring relief from my pain but only highlighted the reality of who God is compared to who I am.

My personal journey is not often the kind we brag about but has been filled with doubt, darkness, and a continual questioning of my own growth. It is often much easier to grasp what we think we know than to talk about the confusion and darkness that we can feel when being led by God. But in opening to this, we can find ourselves on the road to Damascus with Paul, whose run-in with Jesus (the Light of the World) left him in total darkness. Or in a similar way, we find ourselves like Jesus, who after following God's plan the best way he could, cried out, "My God, My God, why have You forsaken Me?" (Matt. 27:46). In fact, when looking through the biblical witness, we are often much more like our brothers and sisters in the faith when we cry out to God, not knowing where he is leading, but turning to the Spirit and trusting that he will lead even if we don't know where.

In 1 Corinthians 2:14–15, Paul states, "But a natural man does not accept the things of the Spirit of God, for they are foolishness to him; and he cannot understand them, because they are spiritually appraised. But he who is spiritual appraises all things." As Christians, we are called to be spiritual—not in an esoteric sense, but in *how we see reality*. Being spiritual, in this sense, is coming to see the way God would have us see. Being spiritual means finding one's view of reality in the Spirit of God rather than in one's own flesh.

> Christianity is not a religion that merely has things for us to accomplish or do but is in fact a religion that calls us to a path of *becoming.*

While God's Spirit is given to us out of love and the desire to commune with us, there is further purpose to it as well. We are not called to communion with God for our purposes but for his. It is in our everyday life that we are called to live by the Spirit so that we may bear fruit in a fruitless world. As one scholar put it, "The purpose of the Spirit's coming was not to transport one above the present age, but to empower one to live within it."[17] God has always been working within each generation to develop a people who will follow and live according to his ways—not the ways of the world, but the way from the Spirit within.

Christianity is not a religion that merely has things for us to accomplish or do but is in fact a religion that calls us to a path of *becoming*. It is only on this path that we can live out kingdom values and actions. This is true, and it could only be true because of the Holy Spirit and the work he does within us. In learning to rely on the Spirit for our way of viewing the world, our source for strength, and our guide in all of life, we are living out a Jesus way of life.

Life in the Spirit is learning to grow, learn, and submit to the God who prays for, guides, and deconstructs our being from the inside out. We have a God who searches the depths of our hearts and who knows how we really see the world, ourselves, and him. We do an injustice to God and others if we fail to live in honesty about who we really are and how we really see things. Life in the Spirit is a life of honesty, humility, and growth.

In this way, life in the Spirit is a lot like life as a child. Parents quickly come to see that children have a natural disposition to see everything based on themselves—they are the center of their known universe. Parents do more than just force the child to do what the parents want; they have the role of guiding the child to a proper understanding of the ways of the world and to an understanding that the child is not the center of the universe. In the same way, the Spirit parents us in growth, guiding us to a life lived well.

It is this life by the Spirit that Thomas R. Kelly called "Life from the Center." Life from the center is living a life led by the Spirit inside of us. As Kelly puts it: "Life from the Center is a life of unhurried peace and power. It is simple. It is serene. It is amazing. It is triumphant. It is radiant. It takes no time, but it occupies all our time. And it makes our life programs new and overcoming. We need not get frantic. He is at the helm. And when our little day is done we lie down quietly in peace, for all is well."[18]

When living by the indwelling Spirit of God, one's life will naturally bear good fruit and will come to adhere to the kingdom way of life. It is by the personal Spirit of the Living God within us that we learn to rightly see the kingdom values in the world. In him we find the wellspring of life, the source of right living walking with us. In order to journey well, we have to come to grips with the mysterious, vast, and overwhelming reality that the Creator of the universe has made a home in our hearts and that he has a purpose for being there.

A Spiritual Priority

It is important to note at this point that the Spirit, as God, is vastly more worthy and important than the other two worldview informers. This might come as a surprise in light of how central the Bible is to the Christian faith. The important distinction is one of kind, not one of clarity.[19] The Spirit is a person of the everlasting God, who took part in creating the Bible and who works through it. The Spirit, because of who he is, automatically becomes the most central of the worldview informers.

This issue is similar to much of what Jesus clashed against when he interacted with the Jewish leadership. Things like the law, the temple, and the nation became the focus of their religious life, over against the commands of God to love, bless, and be holy. Humanity has the tendency to put gifts from God ahead of God himself, whether they are his Word or law, a building or temple, or even his grace or forgiveness. All things should point to God and not become ends in and of themselves, even when he is the giver of these gifts.

Yet because of the nature of the Spirit, we have a much harder time sifting through our own misconceptions, feelings, and thoughts to hear from him. The biblical text becomes a filter for how the Spirit works so that we can hear and discern him. It is of immense importance, though, that we do not pit the Spirit and the Bible against each other, vying for authority. The Spirit took part in creating the Bible, so we must acknowledge the Bible's authority, and the Spirit works within the boundaries described in the Bible (his character, disposition, etc.), even though those boundaries are often vague and without much explanation.

> The Christian life as a whole must be seen with an increasingly spiritual understanding, not merely a natural one.

In all we do, we must keep in mind that our natural inclination will be to make the Spirit into the kind of Spirit *we* want to exist. Often our views of power, strength, or giftedness are vastly different than God's, so we must humbly admit that we do not yet see as we should and submit our views to God for reworking. The Christian life as a whole must be seen with an increasingly spiritual understanding, not merely a natural one.

It would have been awesome to see the Red Sea parted, the pillar of fire, or someone raised from the dead. Acts of power (or "miracles," in more common terminology) still occur in many places, and I have no doubt that God continues to work in this way. But I imagine that for him, these things aren't that impressive. In God's economy, redemption and love are the acts of power that are most valuable, and yet they are the very acts that we rarely find impressive. At my church we recently saw a couple who had been separated for three years come to know the Lord and renew their marriage, bringing their family back together under one roof. That is an act of power that, as far as I'm concerned, is much more impressive than a pillar of fire. The work of the Spirit, while always miraculous, will most often be moving toward works of redemption and reconciliation. We need to see these acts as powerful movements of the Spirit.

Typically, as I have found, people with a naturalistic worldview can easily explain away miracles, and so these acts of power rarely lead to true commitment.[20] But our culture does not know what to do with marriages that are healthy, children who grow in knowledge and maturity, and lives that are redeemed into a unified community of believers. Those are the miracles that our world has no answer for, and these are the brightest lights to a world in darkness.

In light of this, we must never cease to be in awe of the fact that God is with us, as close to us as is possible, by residing in our hearts. As was put beautifully at the assembly of the World Council of Churches in 1968:

> Without the Holy Spirit
> God is far away.
> Christ stays in the past,
> the Gospel is simply an organization,
> authority a matter of propaganda,
> the liturgy is no more than an evolution,
> Christian loving a slave morality.
>
> But in the Holy Spirit,
> the cosmos is resurrected and grows
> with the birth pangs of the Kingdom,
> the Risen Christ is there,
> the Gospel is the power of life,
> the Church shows forth the life of the Trinity,
> authority is a liberating science,
> mission is a Pentecost,
> the liturgy is both renewal and anticipation,
> human action is deified.[21]

We can now live with the Spirit guiding, acting, and honing our worldviews so we can understand that we are now Spirit-people. That changes everything. Because of this fact, a day should never grow dull. But days will inevitably grow dull, which is why we must renew our understanding of the reality that God is still in the business of coming down and hanging out with us.

As a person, the Spirit will not grow us forcefully or without our consent, but he patiently urges that we hand our lives, hearts, and views of reality over to him. As in marriage, this growth may at times feel like regression or bring about frustration and depression, but the goal is not our happiness—it is our holiness.

Spiritual writers all seem to use the same analogy when talking about life with the Spirit: the analogy of marriage. This is interesting in light of the fact that most of these writers were monks and nuns, knowing nothing of marriage in their own lives. There seems to be something fundamentally parallel in the act of two becoming one and the act of the Spirit coming to dwell in our hearts.

In the same way as we grow in love with a spouse, we grow in love with the Spirit. We do not control love, nor do we have the ability to make it happen by forcing our will upon our significant other. It is inevitably reciprocal. Likewise, growth in marriage does not happen by one member going off on his or her own to develop as an individual, trying to grow the marriage through personal effort; it has to be relational and communal. With the Spirit, we must engage in a life of interaction, submission, and an understanding that our growth will not be done on our own but through his power and agenda.

In many parallel ways, seeing our relationship with the Spirit as a dance may help make this reality concrete. The

Spirit leads, but that does not mean we can just drag our feet and expect to dance; we have to learn to follow, develop as a partner, and grow in our understanding of the kind of dancing that the Spirit will lead us in.

6

COMMUNITY

Mirrors and Conduits

I have a good friend who broke up with his long-term girl-friend. After several years of becoming more and more convinced that they weren't good together, he decided to call it quits. After a month though, he seemed to forget any trouble they had ever had and could only remember the love, the good feelings, and the few moments of health. It was as if someone had broken into his mind and removed all of the memories of the fights, the pain, and the incompatibility.

In similar ways, people have a tendency to see the past through rose-colored glasses. With the sounds of melancholy in our voices, we often muse about times that were more peaceful, more fulfilling, and often more meaningful. For some, the focus may be childhood, for others their college days. In any case it seems that all the negative aspects of those memories have been left behind, and all that remains are warm thoughts of times past when "things were the way they should be."

This fascination with "the good ol' days" isn't restricted to personal perspective; it affects the church as well. Many believers tend to look back to the early church with a fondness and fascination, longing for days to be like that again. We see the first-century church as the purest form of church, and we see the growth, missions, and strength it had despite every possible force against it. We see the church we are not, and we want what they had. But in our efforts to recapture the ways of the early church, we are open to any church movement that has the latest and greatest ideas. We look backward and forward seeking the answer to the same question: "How do we make this work?" In the church, we must see *good fruit* for what it is: the natural (well, supernatural) result of a good tree, a healthy church. So the fruit we see in a church—whether it is growth, volunteers, or missions—is fruit that has developed because the church is healthy.[1] This health comes only from abiding in Christ. Yet, in seeking to find answers, we often try to mimic the bearing of fruit and hope that the same effect will take place, and we are confused when it fails to do so.

I grew up at Willow Creek Community Church, and for a summer job I worked on its website. For some reason, anyone with an odd question got forwarded to my phone, and so I tried to respond to such issues as: "What kind of carpet do you use?" "Do you have a cappuccino machine? What kind?" "How can I get last week's message in manuscript form?

Can I have it today? I need to preach this weekend." These questions were from other churches; usually from pastors who desperately wanted to know how to make things work. They saw something they wanted—growth, excitement, enthusiasm, whatever—and they tried to mimic external and oftentimes insignificant aspects of what Willow Creek was doing. It often appears that we have no idea how to *become* good trees, so we just try hard to look like one; it is no wonder everyone knows something is wrong.

To be honest, I am often the guy who is fondly looking back, hoping that we can one day get back to the kind of church the earliest Christians had. But I want to avoid looking at the externals. I don't think it will help us to take the forms they used and apply them in our culture. Instead, we have to take their ideology and apply it to our hearts.

In all the talk about creating community, the answer always seems to be external. We need neighborhood-based small groups, demographic-based home churches, and so on. We also talk as if our only problem is that we don't spend enough time together, but this is only a result of our worldview. The problem of not spending enough time together stems from a deep belief a person has about reality. Just changing the amount of time a person spends with other people will not change that individual's worldview; it will only change behavior. We are still fiddling with the branches of the tree and leaving the roots alone.

OUR FAMILY RESEMBLANCE

When trying to get to know someone, one of the first questions we ask is "What do you do?" What we *do* is, of course, our job, and that information somehow helps people know us better. Sadly, we ask this question because it is how we tend to identify ourselves, not by what we believe, what we value, or what we have given our life to, but by where we work. It is also how we tend to categorize other people.

Likewise, we often ask, "What kind of church do you go to?" This question, like the one above, is really asking, "What form of church do you attend?" or maybe even, "What form of church service do you go to?" These questions say a lot about what we think the church is. We assume that if we know how the church service runs, what the church's priorities are, or even how rooted the church is in history, we will somehow be able to fit that church into a category. Our questions say a lot about what we think a church is; we talk of church very similarly to the way we talk about malls, clubs, and businesses. How many go to your church? How many employees do you have? Do you have a Sears in your mall? Does your church have anything for singles? How much does it cost to be a member of the Lions Club? What do I have to do to become a member of this church?

In contrast, the earliest Christians saw themselves most fundamentally as a family. As expressed by pastor and theologian Joseph Hellerman, "For Jesus . . . family is not one among a variety of equally significant metaphors upon which he draws in order to portray the community he envisions. Rather, it is the dominant social model as well as a metaphor that Jesus uses to engender a specific kind of behavior."[2] Theologian D. G. McCartney writes the following about the importance of family for the ancient world as opposed to today: "Psychologically, a person's identity, from that of the householder to that of the slave, resided in his or her connection to, responsibilities toward and function within a household."[3] In contrast, we in North America tend to see ourselves as fundamentally individual; we find our identity in who we are, what we do, and how we behave. The vision of life we hold to as modern Westerners runs contrary to a familial understanding of Christianity. Christianity is a path toward greater dependency on God and his people and not toward greater individuality.

Here I admit to having a slight advantage. As you might expect, given my last name, I am rarely known as "Kyle" but much more frequently as "Kyle, Lee's son." Because of the way people run those words together, some folks have thought my middle name was Leeson! My identity has always been attached to someone else, and this is precisely how it would have been in the ancient world.

Understanding the worldview of Jesus and the earliest Christians will help us understand their ideology and, therefore, their effectiveness in community. It is also important to note that this kind of worldview is still prevalent in many parts of the world, if not typically in North America. One of the characteristics that defines these groups, and those of the ancient world in particular, is that family is determined first and foremost by bloodlines. "People in collectivist cultures," writes Hellerman, "view family not primarily in terms of *relationship* but in terms of *consanguinity*, that is, in terms of a blood connection with a common ancestor."[4] A similar approach to family by many modern-day ethnic groups can help the rest of us make sense of why they tend to have stronger family ties and tend to be closer to their extended family than those of us in the typical North American family.

As the center of society in the ancient world, family was naturally a focal point of Jesus's teaching. But because of how differently family was viewed then compared to now, we can miss the revolutionary overtones of what Jesus was saying. When Jesus asks, "Who is My mother and who are My brothers?" (Matt. 12:48), we have to see that as an extremely loaded and troubling question to an ancient Jew. Likewise, we often miss Paul's points in Romans and Galatians (which we'll look at below) because we fail to realize that many of the Jews still saw themselves as Abraham's children and, therefore, believed themselves to already have whatever salvation promise they needed.[5] They were within Abraham's bloodline and, therefore, his sons and daughters.

> In any discussion of community, the concept of family must be the axis upon which all other concepts revolve.

When Paul says that "it is those who are of faith who are sons of Abraham" (Gal. 3:7), we should see that as a direct attack on the worldview of that day. Likewise, when John the Baptist proclaims that God can raise up sons of Abraham from stones (Luke 3:8), John is claiming more than that God could re-create a Jew from a stone. John, Jesus, and Paul offer up a worldview-deconstructing thought: it is not bloodline but faith that makes you a child of Abraham and, therefore, within the family of God.

Many people have argued that we misused Jesus's teachings by turning them into a religion. While I understand the thought behind this position, it needs to be applied to Judaism as well. Judaism came from a family comprised of the children of Abraham (as well as any who were adopted into the family), who were in a covenant relationship with God. Jesus was reorienting the Jewish understanding of the covenant to teach that the ones who are truly Abraham's descendants are *the faithful*. The children of faith are in the line of Abraham, and they are the ones with the new covenant promises. Paul then picks up where Jesus left off and makes the point that Abraham himself was the father of faithfulness, and so those who are his children will carry on this family trait (see Romans 4; Galatians 3–4).

In any discussion of community, the concept of family must be the axis upon which all other concepts revolve. If this fails to happen, we'll miss Jesus's reorientation. Jesus was taking a central aspect of the ancient worldview and casting a new vision for their old orientation. In our case, the ancient meaning of *family* doesn't translate very well because our term *family* refers to a smaller, closed unit.

Imagine an orphan boy growing up in the institutional orphanages of Eastern Europe, who only knew family life as institutional life. If this child heard Jesus talk about "hating" your mother and father and wife and children (Luke 14:26), he would fail to feel the offensiveness of his words. He might find this passage odd and out of place, but he wouldn't be able to hear Jesus with the strength of his original point. Likewise, we today have to struggle to understand Jesus on this point. Unless we understand how deep and pervasive the family was in people's lives, we will have a hard time grasping how radical Jesus's reorientation of the family was for the earliest believers.

In many ways, we are now like that orphan boy. Most of us see family as a small unit, mainly closed off from other family units. To hear Jesus's message, we will need to broaden our understanding of what the biblical model of family looks like. One's identity in the ancient world would go well beyond one's immediate family. This is reflected in Joshua 7:18: "And he brought near his household man by man, and Achan the son of Carmi, son of Zabdi, son of Zerah, of the tribe of Judah, was taken" (ESV). Achan then is known as the son of his father Carmi, of his grandfather Zabdi, and of the clan of Zerah, of the house of Judah.[6] As we come to understand community, we need to think in these terms instead of focusing on the family made up of our siblings and parents. To help us shift our thinking, we'll now look at community in terms of family, clan, tribe, and people.

FAMILY

As indicated above, our notion of *family* has nearly no correspondence to the ancient one, and when talking about community, this becomes a very large problem. As I am breaking it up here, *family* will be the lowest common denominator in reference to community, and it is understood in terms of the fellow believers with whom we intimately commune. This will include the members of the church we attend (which will have several layers to it, as all families do), and within that church, the people to whom we are closest. It is important, however, to avoid thinking this means we have to try and be close to everyone in the church. To try to do so would negate the possibility for true community. On the other hand, we must not disappear in cliques of people whom we find attractive and who share the same ideas, look, and attitude as we do. True community benefits from diversity.

In New Testament times the loyalty of one's family and loyalty to a religion were one and the same. Even today, in many cultures conversion to Christianity is equated with death by one's family. Some cultures hold a funeral service for those who convert. This is the kind of worldview the ancient Jews had. Conversion was not merely a change in Sunday morning agenda or venue (or, in their case, Saturday) but was a total change of identity. Converting would be a direct break with everything that one's family of origin stood for. It is in light of this that we need to hear Jesus say:

> Do not think that I came to bring peace on the earth; I did not come to bring peace, but a sword. For I came to set a

man against his father, and a daughter against her mother, and a daughter-in-law against her mother-in-law; and a man's enemies will be the members of his household. He who loves father or mother more than Me is not worthy of Me; and he who loves son or daughter more than Me is not worthy of Me.

Matthew 10:34–37

Conversion is not merely replacing a certain set of beliefs or customs with new ones; it is changing one's fundamental identity and relationship to all the people in one's life. Until we grasp the depth of the family Jesus was creating, we cannot understand the implications this has for the world. Making Jesus a way of life necessitates seeing God as the true Father from whom our family derives and seeing oneself, more than anything else, as a child in that family.

In reference to the early church, McCartney notes, "Since the church as a whole, as well as in its manifestations in local houses, was regarded as a family, the mutual obligations of its members are thought of in terms of family responsibilities."[7] I have to confess that this doesn't mean much to me. I, like most of my generation, do not naturally think in terms of family responsibility but in terms of my own personal desire for life. I choose who I want to let influence my worldview, and they are often very much like me.

Like the disciples, I often have an overly solidified view of how things should be, and I try to force God to work within the limits I set while neglecting to adhere to his. We need to have our views of the church deconstructed by the Spirit. We need to have our family story retold to us in the depths of our hearts so that we might be able to see our new siblings in a new light.

The problem is that, unlike the Bible and the Spirit, we don't automatically trust community. It is not within our tradition to do so. And while we don't usually neglect community completely, which is dangerous and will inevitably distort one's growth, there are several ways that we can be in community but still hinder its work in our lives. First, we can fill our community with people who look like us in their social and cultural makeup and who therefore usually have a worldview that is very similar to ours. Second, because these people are our friends, we can avoid being truthful with each other so as not to step on anyone's toes. Third, because we are so bad at offering truth, when someone *does* speak truth we either view it as an attack or simply dismiss it rather than see it as an act of a true friend.

If we're going to have true community, we need to be open to being in a family that isn't filled with people just like us. Sadly, though, as I look around I see most of the people in my generation doing just that—seeking out what is comfortable, familiar, and nonthreatening. In doing so we make two major mistakes: (1) We neglect the work *God wants to do* in our hearts through our corporate community, and (2) We neglect the work that *brothers and sisters who differ from us* can do in our hearts.

A friend of mine grew up in inner-city Chicago. We met in college, when he arrived at the mostly white, suburban Baptist school we attended. Before long we were really close friends, and even though we had entirely different ways of seeing the world, different tendencies, values, behaviors, and cultural distinctions, we learned to help each other grow and develop as believers. I have had few relationships that caused me to open up how narrow, naive, and arrogant my worldview was than with my friend Jose.

I believe the difference was that our relationship formed the bedrock of our interaction. We were brothers. We both approached each other knowing that while our skin color, the fine points of our theology, and our cultural perceptions had little to nothing in common with each other, we had something fundamental to both of us—a relationship with Jesus. In Christ we were brothers, and because of that we found unity. Unfortunately, in a church context those kinds of relationships seem harder and harder to establish.

Our church experience often has much more to do with showing up to a service and doing things than it does with entering into a family. We often don't understand or take seriously what we are entering because we have the luxury of choosing our *family* based on what we do or do not like. I am reminded of a quote from one of my favorite ancient writers, Seneca, a Stoic philosopher writing around the same time as the apostle Paul: "A person who starts being friends with you because it pays him will similarly cease to be friends because it pays him to do so. . . . What is my object in making a friend? To have someone to be able to die for, someone I may follow into exile, someone for whose life I may put myself up as security and pay the price as well. The thing you describe is not friendship but a business deal, looking to the likely consequences, with advantage as its goal."[8]

The same thought can easily be applied to the church today. We are not looking for friendship or family, at least not in any deep sense, but for elation or satisfaction. I'm just as guilty of this as anyone. If the people at my church are really my family, I am not a very good brother. I think about all those I tend to avoid, those I have never bothered meeting, and those I *know of* but have never taken the opportunity to really *know*. But I know that their sin, pain, and brokenness are family concerns, and as a brother I should be deeply involved in their lives trying to help them figure it out.

As J. Ramsey Michaels said, "Only in community . . . is it possible to follow in the path that Jesus walked alone."[9] Only when we truly believe that, will we accept each other as a family. This reality is one that few of us have grasped: that in Christianity, the task of growth is fruitless without the help of others.

We often fail to love one another, choosing instead to be nice to each other, but as every family knows, niceties are a sign of shallowness. Despite all the frustration and struggle that family life can bring, the potential for true growth is without limit. It is the times of frustration and struggle that are conduits for the Spirit to grow, deconstruct, and admonish believers to a deeper walk with him.

A FAMILY FOR THE WORLD

In our call to be brothers and sisters, fathers and mothers, we are called to be a family to the world that has never had one. Jesus came to people with broken lives and broken homes and offered a chance to have fathers who love and do not condemn, mothers who care for and nurture in wisdom, and brothers and sisters who know them deeply and love them anyway. Possibly the reason the New Testament writers focused on family relationships and unity is that family is the central place for redemption. We offer more than conversion to a movement; we offer a family that much of the world is so desperately looking for.

Jean Vanier, the father of the l'Arche communities, says this:

Community is the place where our limitations, our fears and our egoism are revealed to us. We discover our poverty and our weaknesses, our inability to get on with some people, our mental and emotional blocks, our affective or sexual disturbances, our seemingly insatiable desires, our frustrations and jealousies, our hatred and our wish to destroy. . . . An experience in prayer and the experience of being loved and accepted in community, which has become a safe place for us, allows us gradually to accept ourselves as we are, with our wounds and all the monsters. We are broken, but we are loved. We can grow to greater openness and compassion; we have a mission. Community becomes the place of liberation and growth.[10]

> Authentic community is one of the root systems of the tree of kingdom living.

Authentic community is one of the root systems of the tree of kingdom living. Real community, when embodying the Spirit and the Bible as informers, becomes the answer to a world that is broken and in pain. It is the answer because it is the body of Christ and therefore leads to the ultimate answer: Jesus himself. Since *the* Christian family trait is that we love each other, our love needs to be real, authentic, and central to everything that takes place in the church. Too often, living in community and loving each other serves only to satisfy people's emptiness, and that is why the church in many traditions has grown weaker and weaker as each generation has grown more and more individualistic. Community in itself is not the answer, and it can easily become a way to further narcissism.

I tend to err on the side of niceness when it comes to relationships. Usually, it is easy to justify this as the "loving" thing to do, simply because the person doesn't feel bad. In the last several years though, God has brought many people who are the opposite of me into my life—they err on the side of truth-telling, and they consider it the loving thing to do regardless of whether the recipient likes it or not. I have a distinct memory of being in a group as one individual proceeded to explain to another individual exactly how that person was acting—how it was manipulative, self-centered, and clearly a response of trying to cover up that person's own feelings of worthlessness. No one could question that he was right, but all I could do was squirm and try to mentally disappear. But because it was done by someone who was trusted and loved, the person accepted it as truth and was able to open up more fully to his own heart.

In light of this, we shouldn't be surprised when Paul follows up a discussion on living the Christian life (Eph. 4:17–25) with an equally long discourse on living within community (Eph. 4:26–32), saying that we should "speak truth each one of you with his neighbor, for we are members of one another" (Eph. 4:25). The work of the Spirit in the lives of believers takes place, more often than not, within the interactions of the group. We grow as we commune. Because *information* has been the sacred cow of the Protestant tradition, we have minimized the importance of community growth out of fear that the information will be compromised. Sadly, in doing so, the church has allowed the greatest stumbling block to be put in the path of the believer—the demand for growth without the support of community.

It would not be possible, nor helpful, for me to list how a community should function as a family. I think that, while we may not know exactly how this would look in our specific contexts, we do intuitively know what it means. We must enter into the kind of relationships with people that allows them to see our hearts. We need to be people who can speak authoritatively into each other's lives and not merely offer a barrage of Bible verses and Christian clichés. We need to be the kind of community that knows the depths of the ugliness of each other's lives and yet sees each other in love, in trust, and with the heart of a brother or sister.

We see this in Paul's heart for the Thessalonians when he wrote his letter to encourage them to live a godly life. In this affectionate missive to the church he had founded, Paul shows himself to be constantly concerned about them in his heart (i.e., he constantly prayed for them—1 Thess. 1:2). But what stands out most is that Paul is writing to his family. In the second chapter alone, Paul comes to them as a brother (2:1, 9, 14, 17), as an infant (2:7a),[11] as a nursing mother (2:7b), like a father (2:11), and as one orphaned from them (2:17).[12] Paul ends this section by saying, "For what is our hope or joy or crown of boasting before our Lord Jesus at his coming? Is it not you? For you are our glory and joy" (1 Thess. 2:19–20 ESV).

Paul, one of the most important figures in the early church, shows in this letter the depth of his love for his newfound family. As their founder, Paul's love for them is like that of a brother, but he also cared and worried for them like a parent. It is interesting that Paul grounds his letter not only in his familial connection but also in his frequent use of the phrase, "as you know." He tells them how to live by using his own life, which they had seen when he lived among them. So, like a father, Paul can admonish them because *they know how he lived* and therefore also know how they are supposed to live.

While family language can help us understand how important it is to have fellow brothers and sisters who walk with us along the way, it is also important to know how vast our family is. In North American circles, *family* often refers only to the immediate family, but in the biblical understanding of the term, it is much broader than this. Just as we might talk loosely about our second or third cousins as family even though it usually doesn't mean much to us, a biblical understanding of the term includes all believers, regardless of distance or similarity.

CLAN

There is no doubt that the Christian *family*, as I am using it here, will provide the greatest amount of support and guidance in a believer's life, but that does not mean the larger family should be ignored. Your "clan" is the Christian community in whatever city or town you live in—the people of God in a given location. We see this concept in the book of Romans: Paul wrote one letter to the Christian clan in Rome, made up of all the various churches in the city. It can be tempting to think of fellow church members as being "on our team" and members of other churches as being somehow against us. I have seen many churches fail in a ministry endeavor or end up unable to accomplish their goals because they refuse to see the other Christians in their area as part of their same larger family. Likewise, I have seen the majority of the eighteen- to thirty-year-olds in a specific area leave their various churches and flock to the same church, rejecting the concept of a generational family for one filled with people who look, think, and act like them. In our quest for comfort, we often become narrow-minded, isolated, and oblivious to the other Christian *families* around us.

It is easy to see how much we have failed at being a unified clan just by observing how infrequently churches band together to work in unity in their community. As Vanier has noted, "Religious . . . groupings . . . become filled with the desire 'to win,' to beat others, to prove they are right through powerful means. They become blinded by their own concerns and desire for power . . . they are unable to see and appreciate the beauty of others."[13] Churches, like individuals, will end up pursuing their own interests far more than those of the kingdom if they fail to keep the clan in mind.

I've tried to meditate on what it would be like if all of the various Christian groups within a city actually came to view themselves as a family. Instead of being isolated mavericks, the local college ministry would help the church bless students, while the church could help support their workers. Instead of focusing on drawing in a new kind of person (e.g., seekers), maybe the church would fund the efforts of a group of people who feel called to reach out to a particular social group, regardless of whether their own church sees any of the converts begin to attend, and so on. We in the church must come to grips with the reality that we are far more focused on our own church's concerns over against those of the kingdom.

By thinking of ourselves and our fellow believers as the body of Christ of Los Angeles (or London or Cairo or Seoul), our vision will automatically be brought beyond our own congregation and our own desire to *win* or to *be the best*. If we consider our solitary church to be the only body of Christ that knows what it's doing, then we mock the prayer that Jesus prayed for the church: "The glory which You have given Me I have given to them, that they may be one, just as We are one; I in them and You in Me, that they may be perfected in unity, so that the world may know that You sent Me, and loved them, even as You have loved Me" (John 17:22–23).

It is through
our unity
that the world
will know that God
the Father
has sent
Jesus Christ.

It is through our unity that the world will know that God the Father has sent Jesus Christ. That should be a humbling fact—and a worldview-deconstructing statement. Our lack of attention to this area of the body shows how little our vision of life looks like that of Jesus. In this sense the first step to being mission-minded is being community-minded.

The call for unity is certainly needed on a churchwide level, but we can't stop there. Along with considering other churches our partners, we need to do the work of actually partnering with and taking care of them, just as Paul instructed the Romans: "For just as we have many members in one body and all the members do not have the same function, so we, who are many, are one body in Christ, and individually members one of another. . . . Be devoted to one another in brotherly love; give preference to one another in honor" (Rom. 12:4–5, 10). Given Paul's instructions, we can see the Gentiles and the Jews were divided and neglecting their family roles with one another, just like Baptists, Episcopalians, Lutherans, Methodists, Presbyterians, and all the other denominational and nondenominational groups do in every city in North America.

The reality of our failure to be unified, often even in our own congregations, needs to be faced head-on because our disunity is sending an extremely loud message to the world. The church needs to be "the hearing church," to use theologian John Webster's terminology. It is hearing the Word, the Spirit, and others in our community of believers that allows us to grow and develop. In Webster's words: "Through

Scripture the church is constantly exposed to interruption. Being the hearing church is never, therefore, a matter of routine, whether liturgical or doctrinal. It is, rather, the church's readiness 'that its whole life should be assailed, convulsed, revolutionized and reshaped.' "[14] Life in the church is a life of nonstop worldview development, and only by having a unified body will we as a clan be sure to develop our worldviews so that they are unified as well.

TRIBE

When my wife and I were in Scotland recently, my second cousins met us for a day. I had only met my cousins once before and wasn't sure where "second cousins" even fit on the family tree. All I knew was that, according to some distant bloodline, they were family. And even though these roles and distinctions have been neglected in the world that I know, there was still something special about our relationship with them. We were a part of the same group, however distant and removed. We belonged to the same mold, and that meant something.

Likewise, as we are adopted into the family of God, we are adopted into a much larger, more removed group as well: our tribe. Our *tribe*, as I am using it here, consists of both the North American (or substitute the continent where you reside) Christian population and the Christian population of the world.[15] A tribe can also take on various attributes of a family and will have different levels of influence and intimacy. It is because of this tribe mentality that a church in Africa, for example, can be intimately connected to a church in Germany, for example. This is because we are a common tribe, a common people.

There are certainly many levels between the *clan* and the *tribe*; things like state, country, or continent could serve as demarcations. But, like with a family, proximity does not necessarily determine closeness. We need to recognize that distance only demands more strategy and determination to maintain closeness, rather than making it impossible.

In terms of worldview, the tribe is extremely important. In North America we tend to think we know more than those in other countries, as if we are on the "cutting edge of ministry" and are the answer to the world's problems. We tend to make decisions separate from our clan, let alone our tribe. We are members of a worldwide people, and we have brothers and sisters in every nation. That fact should be both awe-inspiring and downright humiliating when we consider the kinds of problems we think we have compared to those of Christians in the developing world. If Paul were to write the Epistle to the Church in the United States, I think he might say:

> Therefore I, the prisoner of the Lord, implore you to walk in a manner worthy of the calling with which you have been called, with all humility and gentleness, with patience, showing tolerance for one another in love, being diligent to preserve the unity of the Spirit in the bond of peace. There is one body and one Spirit, just as also you were called in one hope of your calling; one Lord, one faith, one baptism, one God and Father of all who is over all and through all and in all.
>
> Ephesians 4:1–6

I think he would admonish us to recognize our tribe, our fellow brothers and sisters whom we do not know, reminding us that we are all one in Jesus. I think Paul would also call attention to our lack of unity on even the smallest scale, pointing out that we must be unified in the smallest sections of the community if we want unity as a whole. Along these lines, Vanier states:

"My people" are those who are written in my flesh as I am in theirs. Whether we are near each other or far away, my brothers and sisters remain written within me. I carry them, and they, me; we recognise each other again when we meet. To call them "my people" doesn't mean that I feel superior to them, or that I am their shepherd or that I look after them. It means that they are mine as I am theirs. There is a solidarity between us. What touches them, touches me. And when I say "my people," I don't imply that there are others I reject. My people is my community, made up of those who know me and carry me. They are a springboard towards all humanity. I cannot be a universal brother or sister unless I first love my people.[16]

We also need to understand that, as members of a tribe, every decision we make affects the other members of our tribe. No matter how loosely we are connected, we are still the children of Abraham by faith on whom God has staked his reputation. This fact alone should help us maintain a pliable worldview!

In being of one tribe, we are truly a nation unto ourselves, though we are without boundaries or borders. We are a nation telling the story of who we are in relationship to the world. In doing so, we are separate from the rest of the world because we are telling a different story, and in and through that story we find unity. As a tribe, we need to know our story and find ourselves within the narrative of God's redemptive history of the world.

The mistake we often make is that of failing to make the story a family story, and instead try to make it a story about personal salvation. Our individualism has caused us to think of the gospel in terms of personal salvation alone, which is certainly a major facet, but it is still only *one* facet in the overarching story of the redemption of humankind. That is our story, and the story is being told by our people, for our people, and as we will now see, has been handed down from our people.

> Our individualism has caused us to think of the gospel in terms of personal salvation alone, which is certainly a major facet, but it is still only *one* facet in the overarching story of the redemption of humankind.

PEOPLE

So far we have looked at our family in two-dimensional terms, using geographic distance as our factor of separation. But to understand our family as a people, we must add a third dimension. As the people of God, we are in a deep and vast family tree that extends back to Adam; in essence, we are the newest-born infants in the family of God. If we are to take the task of worldview development seriously, we must take seriously the people who paved the way before us. We must think, live, and be formed by the recognition that we are brothers and sisters of the apostles, the church fathers, the desert mothers and fathers, the saints, the martyrs, and on and on.

Just as it was with Israel, our task is to be the people of God, the descendants of Abraham who are to bless the world. As the people of God, our call is to "be a holy nation [people]" (1 Peter 2:9) under God as a sign to the world showing who our God is. Unlike Israel, the outward manifestations of our Christian community are not land or circumcision but spiritual fruit and love.[17]

We are part of a long tradition of people whom God has sought out in order to come and dwell with them. It is a sad reality that many of us live as though we were the first to try to live according to the Bible, the first to preach, and the first to be a living, healthy, and missional church. To the contrary, we are just the most recent in a long line of spiritual relatives who are walking this path—failing, succeeding, and trying to live the kingdom life.

In many ways, as older relatives in our family see pieces of our ancestors in our features, our personalities, and our idiosyncrasies, we can see pieces of Paul, Luther, Ignatius, Teresa of Avila, and all of the saints who have preceded our time in our desires, struggles, and behaviors. Failing to learn from them is failing to understand who we are, why we act the way we do, and how the kingdom of God has been moving throughout time.

> We are part of a long tradition of people whom God has sought out in order to come and dwell with them.

Understanding our place within our family history helps us in several ways. The past can mirror back our own reality in a way that our present family cannot. Our present family is often either too harsh, which only raises our defenses, or not harsh enough, which means they never point out our blind spots. Figures from the past, on the other hand, can bring to question all of our presuppositions, simply because they did not assume them.

When we read about claims and beliefs held by previous generations that are obviously skewed, we can recognize that, just like them, we hold to facets of our own worldview that are probably a little skewed, too. America's most famous theologian, Jonathan Edwards, thought the pope was the Antichrist and that he could calculate the return of Christ from when the papacy was inaugurated. Instead of rolling our eyes and asking, "How could he possibly believe that?" we can ask ourselves, "What do *we* believe that is dependent upon our worldview and which will cause future believers to roll their eyes at us?"[18]

Since the rise of the seeker/interdenominational movements and on through the current conversation about the emerging church, there has been a free-for-all when it comes to new approaches to the form church takes. I imagine that in the future this time period will be looked at as a necessary reevaluation of the way we do church and a time of rethinking what is more important: the form or the ideology. But even in our culture today, those who broke down the old forms just re-created new ones. In everything we do, it seems that we seek to solidify whatever form it is that we find comfortable.

A friend of mine often muses that the human heart longs to make things *ends* that should only be *means*.[19] I believe one reason for this is that our view of reality is so stunted. We could see with much greater breadth if we would only spend time learning from those before us. In seeing the way our long-departed brothers and sisters worked, studied, worshiped, and lived, we come to understand the world through their eyes and can therefore better critique the way we see the world through our own.

When I was struggling with the feeling that God had left me, I had John of the Cross, an ancient Christian spiritualist, to help me understand what was going on in my life. I weathered my depression and sorrow with the peace of God because I had in him a brother who could explain my situation and help me see where God was in it all. In the words of theologian James Houston,

> Paul prays that we may grasp this limitless love of Christ in company with "all the saints." We need to read the great classics of the Christian faith in order to understand how other Christians have grasped this same love of Christ. . . . We rob ourselves if we do not learn to live with Augustine, Thomas Aquinas, Teresa of Avila, John of the Cross, Martin Luther, Jonathan Edwards, and the whole hosts of the saints who have truly been friends of God.[20]

Those who have walked before us are brothers and sisters along the way, and like our living siblings, they can guide and lead us in our walk with Christ. Along those lines, it is important to know what kind of impact a united people would have on the world, and for this, we can go to the early church. This quote is from a letter written in the second century to a man named Diognetus about the ancient Christian people. This is how the writer described the ancient church:

> For Christians are not differentiated from other people by country, language or customs; you see, they do not live in cities of their own, or speak some strange dialect, or have some peculiar lifestyle. . . . They live in both Greek and foreign cities, wherever chance has put them. They follow local customs in clothing, food, and the other aspects of life. But at the same time, they demonstrate to us the wonderful and certainly unusual form of their own citizenship. They live in their own native lands, but as aliens; as citizens they share all things with others; but like aliens, suffer all things. Every foreign country is to them as their native country, and every native land as a foreign country. They marry and have children just like everyone else; but they do not kill unwanted babies. They offer a shared table, but not a shared bed. They are at present "in the flesh" but they do not live "according to the flesh." They are passing their days on earth, but are citizens of heaven. They obey the appointed laws, and go beyond the laws in their own lives. They love everyone, but are persecuted by all. They are unknown and condemned; they are put to death and gain life. They are poor and yet make many rich. They are short of everything and yet have plenty of all things. They are dishonored and yet gain glory through dishonor. Their names are blackened and yet they are cleared. They are mocked and bless in return. They are treated outrageously and behave respectfully to others. When they do good, they are punished as evildoers; when punished, they rejoice as if

being given a new life. They are attacked by Jews as aliens, and are persecuted by the Greeks; yet those who hate them cannot give any reason for their hostility. To put it simply—the soul is to the body as Christians are to the world. The soul is spread through all parts of the body and Christians through all the cities of the world. The soul is in the body but is not of the body; Christians are in the world but not of the world.[21]

> Our hope to be a light to the world depends on how seriously we take community.

The goal of community is never community itself but a greater knowledge, trust, and love of God. Our hope to be a light to the world depends on how seriously we take community. It is through the various levels of community that we can come to understand how blind we often are to our own presuppositions and assumptions about the world, about the church, or even about our place in history. It is unfortunate that North Americans are seen by the world to be self-consumed and arrogant, and it is a greater tragedy that North American Christians can often be seen this way by the rest of our tribe.

In living the community life, we must start off in our own group of friends and our immediate family in Christ. Honesty with and among our siblings will be the first step toward a real community environment that extends through space and time. The more I meditate on the idea of community, the more I am drawn to believe that life isn't long enough to live in shallow community; it just isn't worth it. We have a world that needs to hear the message of Jesus, and our greatest opportunity to spread this message is through the power of the redemption and reconciliation of people.

7

SELFVIEW

Narcissus Reimagined

Like most of my generation, when I left the church of my youth I was angry, bitter, and frustrated. I felt those emotions were not only justified but righteous. Since that time, through my own honesty with the Bible, the Spirit, and fellow believers, I have come to see that my emotions said much more about *me* than they did about how justified my anger was. I see now how the decisions I made for several years after leaving the church stemmed from feeling abused, neglected, and unnoticed.

I now know that my problem wasn't about truth; it was about perspective. I still think I was justified in feeling those things—the church did in fact let me down. But that wasn't the issue. My frustrations had more to do with the fact that I believed I deserved more, that I was more important than how I'd been treated, and that the church deserved to be bashed because of that. It is a sad commentary on the church that my generation feels this way, but it is also a testimony about my generation that many of us have continued in our anger toward the church for so many years and have even started churches or other organizations because of our anger.

My purpose here is not to discuss the problems in the church, which have led to many factions and individual frustrations, but to discuss the individual: the lowest common denominator of the Christian faith and the place where we all start. Up until this point, I have talked around the concept of the individual, particularly because this is the element that is most often discussed in our individualistic culture. But for the purpose of this chapter, I want us to look at how the individual relates to the task of worldview development.

In a sense, there is a fourth worldview informer, and it is the self. The concept of selfview involves two different issues: First, what do we believe, and how do we know we believe those things? Second, how do the various worldview informers help to inform who we really are and how we see reality? In this sense then, *selfview* is about knowing yourself, knowing what you believe, and knowing what it means to have those things formed into the likeness of Christ.

It can't be emphasized enough how important it is to have an accurate view of yourself. Having an accurate selfview enables you to respond appropriately to Jesus, his Word, his Spirit, and the community he has formed. It is in this light that we must remember Peter falling at Jesus's feet and proclaiming, "Go away from me Lord, for I am a sinful man, O Lord!" (Luke 5:8). Peter is not at all delusional about who he is or how righteous (or, in this case, unrighteous) he is;

because of his self-understanding he is able to respond to Jesus in honesty and humility.

Likewise, the woman who anoints Jesus with perfume and kisses Jesus's feet (Luke 7:37–50) is said to love much because she has been forgiven much, and the one who is forgiven little (presumably the Pharisee in whose house they were eating) is said to love little. This passage is often quoted to show that those who are down-and-out and *really* need help will appreciate Jesus's offer more. While this may be true in a general sense, I think Jesus's point has much more to do with one's self-understanding. If the Pharisees truly knew themselves, and how deeply wicked their hearts were (see Jer. 17:9), they would have responded in the same way as the woman, but as Jesus notes, their actions say everything about how much they think they need forgiveness.

While the idea of selfview can be found in the New Testament, it has been a part of our modern tradition as well (although we have failed to talk much about it lately). Calvin starts off his work, *Institutes of the Christian Religion*, saying, "Nearly all the wisdom we possess, that is to say, true and sound wisdom, consists of two parts: the knowledge of God and of ourselves."[1] Much further back, in approximately AD 200, Clement of Alexandria stated, "It is then, as appears, the greatest of all lessons to know one's self."[2] From the beginning of the Christian faith, it has been a value to know oneself, and to know oneself truly.

This may shed light on the sin of pride and the virtue of humility. The prideful person is ignorant of both who God is and, therefore also, who he or she is. On the other hand, the humble person is merely agreeing with what should be obvious to the Christian—without God, he or she can do nothing (John 15:5). The call to humility and the call away from pride, therefore, are not a summons to or away from something but guidance toward right seeing.

> We affirm the relational side of Christianity and then go on doing church, neglecting to learn how to relate with God on an intimate level.

As we've already discussed, seeing yourself rightly is the first step toward right living. According to Martin Luther: "A man should know himself, should know, feel, and experience that he is guilty of sin and subject to death; but he should also know the opposite, that God is the Justifier and Redeemer of a man who knows himself this way."[3] Knowing oneself, then, is the first step in conversion (the recognition of the need for forgiveness), and it is *a constant step for growth* in the Christian life.[4]

In order to get a better grasp of what selfview is, particularly in terms of worldview development, we need to focus on our beliefs. The typical convert, like the individual who grows up in the church, receives instruction by being told "what Christians believe." The person is then forced to learn this information, which usually entails memorization, because they are now "in the faith" and need to learn the tenets of the faith. At first glance, there doesn't seem to be much wrong with this picture, but I hope that soon it will be apparent how inadequate this really is.

It is often said that Christianity is a "relationship, not a religion," and yet it seems that no one has any idea what exactly that means. We affirm the relational side of Christianity and then go on doing church, neglecting to learn how to relate with God on an intimate level. Even the way we talk about this relationship is suspect. How can we learn what it means to grow with God relationally when the way we teach and preach about it fails to be relational? As noted by James M. Houston, even our belief that God is personal is communicated in an impersonal way.[5] More often than not, the evangelical church has talked from the pulpit, which fails to be personal or relational, about a personal and relational God. In the end, unfortunately, beliefs about this relationship are changed by chance alone, and the church has done little to help model what Christianity as a relationship actually looks like.

WHAT DOES IT MEAN TO BELIEVE?

When talking about what it means to believe something, Dallas Willard offers two definitions: "To believe is a readiness to act as if something were so," and "What you believe is what you act as if it were true."[6] The two together help to show that what we believe is acted out in what we do. A belief, then, will lead to either action or acceptance, depending on the belief in question. For instance, I can't really act on my belief that the planet Jupiter is round, but I accept it and would act on that belief if given the opportunity to do so. And when we believe something to be true, we must act according to that reality. For someone to say that they truly believe they have won the lotto, but at the same time claim that they refuse to look at their ticket, clearly shows that they do not believe it to be true.[7]

I started to have something like a gag reflex when I first began to think about linking my beliefs with action. For most of my life I had subconsciously separated these two things so I wouldn't have to deal with the consequences. Unfortunately, I had come to think about beliefs as statements that I either affirmed or denied, and judged them based on how they made me feel (warm, frustrated, annoyed, etc.). So, for instance, I believe that it is good for me and my body to eat vegetables, but I also feel very negatively about that specific belief (because I hate them!).[8] I usually live by the deeper belief underlying all of this: that I should be able to eat whatever I want (a belief I am almost never honest about or vocalize, and possibly a belief I don't even realize I have).

However, beliefs are much more complex than simple statements. Using my vegetable example, we'd say that the first belief, that vegetables are good for me, is a conscious belief. Basically, a conscious belief is a belief that we can affirm relatively quickly when asked about it ("Do you believe in gravity?"). These are beliefs we have thought about before and, in the case of many of them, we have actually thought through and picked the side we believe to be true (e.g., "Does God exist?" "Will the Lakers ever win a title again?" "Should we have gone to war?") or which we just naturally believe (e.g., gravity, our sex, etc.).

Our conscious beliefs will be both beliefs that we have accepted ("I accept that food is important") and that we live on ("Therefore, I eat"). But what about beliefs that we hold but don't live by, like when we say "speeding is wrong," but then continue going 80 m.p.h. in a 65 m.p.h. zone? In this case we'd say we either have other beliefs that are more central to our belief structure,[9] or else we have deeper hidden desires and beliefs that we may not be able to put into words. These beliefs may be something like, "I can do anything I want," "If I have a desire, I can act on it without consequence," and so forth.[10] We don't like these beliefs to be known, so we hide them, but they are the beliefs that we act on in every situation in which we find ourselves. We do not normally put these kinds of beliefs into words, but they make up the way we intuitively live; they are our unconscious beliefs. We don't talk about these; we just act on them. They are the hidden belief systems that run our lives.

When an unconscious belief is exposed to us, we will often respond defensively by explaining our behavior away or by retelling our reality through a story where that kind of action would make sense. In other words, we are often more surprised than others when we realize that we believe these things. The degree to which we are surprised by our unconscious beliefs is the degree to which we do not know ourselves[11] and are probably living very differently than what we affirm to be true.

A good example of our two kinds of beliefs is shown through the movie *The Shawshank Redemption*. In the movie, the prisoners clearly have the belief (like all would) that prison is a bad place to be. This belief is a conscious belief that they were able to spend a good deal of their lives contemplating. However, the unconscious belief that some held about prison did not come out until they were released. This belief was that the institution was the safest place to be and the world was too different, too fast-paced, and too scary.

Brooks, the character in the movie who gets paroled, writes back to his former fellow inmates and tells them:

> I have trouble sleeping at night; I have bad dreams like I'm falling. I wake up scared. Sometimes it takes me a while to remember where I am. Maybe I should get me a gun and rob the Food Way so they'd send me home. I could shoot the manager while I was at it, sorta like a bonus. I guess I'm too old for that sorta nonsense anymore. I don't like it here, I'm tired of being afraid all the time. I've decided not to stay. I doubt they'd kick up any fuss, not for an old crook like me.[12]

Even though Brooks spent his whole time in prison thinking about getting out, when he was finally out he was able to realize that prison was home; it was the place he felt safe, where his friends were, and where he understood how life worked. Somewhere along the line Brooks came to be afraid of "normal" life and found the prison system to be safe and comfortable.

The problem the characters of the movie faced, and that we face as well, is that it is impossible for us to change our beliefs. This may sound counterintuitive, but think about it. Could you really stop believing that you exist, that you are a particular sex, that you are a particular ethnicity, or other such beliefs? No, you cannot, in the same way that Brooks couldn't stop and say to himself, "Wow, I'm free, I guess I'll stop feeling afraid now." Brooks's feeling of fear was a natural outcome of his subconscious beliefs about reality. What he could do, and what we can do, is to put ourselves in a position to have that belief changed (through research, a new point of view, etc.). Usually we just act as if we believe it, without ever really coming to believe it is true. We change our behavior but leave our old beliefs intact. We attack belief transformation just like the Pharisees, who seemed to believe that, "If we act rightly, then we will believe rightly."

In terms of the convert then, we have a problem. Take, for example, a young man who comes to believe in Jesus and then is told that he believes x, y, and z. Does he believe these things? Probably not. He's being told that all Christians affirm these statements and so he should do the same. Frustration occurs when his actions show otherwise, and he doesn't understand why telling himself these beliefs over and over doesn't make them any more true for him.

On the other hand, consider the young woman who grew up in a Christian home. She assumes these beliefs in her worldview, but she tends to only acknowledge the statements and fails to take seriously the task of belief transformation. She was never forced to question her belief in them because she was constantly surrounded by others who affirmed them as well, so her beliefs had no reason to change. In both the convert and the person born into a Christian household, it is much easier for people to change behavior and leave their fundamental beliefs unchanged.

> We have no idea what we *really* believe.

Prayer is a good example for this type of thing. When I discovered that I didn't believe prayer worked, it was a surprise because I never would have questioned it. If someone had asked me point blank, "Do you believe that prayer works?" I would have affirmed it wholeheartedly. *Of course I do!* This brings us to a disconcerting dilemma. We have no idea what we *really* believe.

During my personal enlightenment, I came to understand the point that New Testament theologian William Barclay makes: "One of the great neglected duties of the Christian life is self-examination, and maybe self-examination is neglected because it is so humiliating an exercise."[13] But this was certainly more than humiliating; here I was, a lifelong Christian who was now a Biblical Studies major, involved in leadership and ministry, and *I didn't believe prayer worked.* But through this discovery I was able to find what the ancient writers knew: that knowing oneself is a necessary step to knowing God, and knowing God necessitates knowing oneself.

Coming to see this about myself was devastating. I was not arrogant enough to think that I had it all together, but I certainly thought I was further along than this! It was during this time that the ideas of God being living water, light, and love really hit me. These were not just things that you can

> We cannot change what we believe, but we can be in community, in the Spirit, in the Bible, and aware of ourselves enough to offer up our beliefs for change.

experience, but things you are "in." I also started to notice Paul's language about being "in" Jesus and started to understand that our growth has to occur "in" something.

Just as we have to be reborn, and metaphorically go back "in" to the womb, we have to have our beliefs changed "in" something. We cannot change what we believe, but we can be in community, in the Spirit, in the Bible, and aware of ourselves enough to offer up our beliefs for change. Just as we can't get a suntan by thinking hard about it but have to be "in the light," we cannot believe rightly until we are "in the love of God." In order to have that environment be healthy and guided, we need to be guided by Jesus, with the staff of the worldview informers, as sheep are guided by a shepherd.

One of our problems is that, while it is not possible to change our beliefs just by thinking hard, it *is* possible to self-deceive. Self-deception, for our purposes, is when we become so inundated with a conscious belief that we fail to see our unconscious beliefs. For Christians, this is a serious reality. Saying the "right" thing has become an art form for Christians. We see it at all levels, from the pastors who commit adultery and the leaders who want people to do what they say but not what they do, to the congregants who do all the church tells them to and have no idea why it isn't working.

I know what you're probably wondering: Is it *really* possible for us to have *no idea* what we believe? I don't want to overstate my point, so I will say we *can* know, but we must be constantly suspicious of ourselves in the process. Our problem is that if we do examine ourselves, we too easily respond to our examination with Christian cliché answers or with what we wish we actually did believe. Since the examination of ourselves will uncover many painful self-realizations, we must find our comfort in Jesus and the fact that he knows everything we really believe and loves us anyway. This is what is hard about writing this in a book: As readers, you can easily nod your heads in agreement and go on, never really opening up to the reality of what you really believe.

In order to help us figure out what we really believe, there are some questions we can ask ourselves as a way to examine our hearts. What is important is that we *do not* answer these questions ourselves but that we allow our lives to answer for us. Take some time to look back at the past week (or a typical week in your life) and allow your actions and activities to answer the following questions:

1. How did I spend my time? How much, and to what extent, did the worldview informers play a part in my life, compared to things like television, the Internet, and entertainment in general? What does my time spent tell me about what I believe to be true about the world and reality? What made me angry, sad, happy, anxious, lonely, and fearful? What do my emotions tell me about what I believe? (For example, I have found that a central belief I have is that I should never be cut off on the freeway, and I justify my anger as righteous because of that.)

2. What did my prayer life look like? How often did I pray to or think about God? Are there any areas of my life that I did not share with God, or are there areas I find uncomfortable to talk about with God? What do my prayer life and my feelings about prayer tell me about what I believe about God? (For example, my prayer has

lately had to do with how little I want to pray. I find it easier to do work than to talk with God, which points very clearly to where I tend to find my identity.)
3. What is my private thought life like? What do I daydream about? Is there a lifestyle that I find myself coveting? If I could daydream about "the good life," what would it be, and would I refer to it as a *Christian* way to see the world? Why or why not? (I remember daydreaming about being a professional athlete and coming to realize that I believed that was the good life.)
4. If I could imagine God showing up and saying something to me, what would he say? What do I assume God feels when I come to mind?[14] (I sometimes worry that God won't show up at all, which is the very thing I should be talking with him about.)

As you can see, these aren't questions we can ask just once and then stick in a drawer—asking them should be a regular discipline in the Christian life. And they don't have to be these specific questions, although I think these are a good place to start; they can be any questions that help your life speak your beliefs.

What we need to do is develop a discipline that helps us to see our true beliefs for what they are. A. W. Tozer says, "Were we able to extract from any man a complete answer to the question, 'What comes into your mind when you think about God?' we might predict with certainty the spiritual future of that man."[15] His point is that we naturally live out our beliefs, whether we acknowledge them or not. Therefore the beliefs about who we are and who God is determine how we respond to, live out, and internalize the Christian faith.

As I've gone around the country speaking at various colleges, churches, and events, I ask people some or all of these questions and find some similarities:

First, when these questions are asked, people have a really hard time being honest with themselves about these things. It's as though they have pretended to be something else for so long that they have shut down in their minds the possibility that something else might be true. As we'll see below, community is going to be central to the task of bringing these things to light.

> What we need to do is develop a discipline that helps us to see our true beliefs for what they are.

Second, people are amazed that the doctrines they affirm in church rarely make it into their lives. Everywhere I go, people can relate to my story about not believing that prayer works. Over and over again I hear how much that story speaks to people's hearts, which shows me that the church has done a poor job of helping people come to true believing so that it affects their lives and not merely their statements (which is often referred to as their "heads"). There is often not a safe place where people can be honest about who they are, and that comes from the church caring more about the look of holiness than its reality.

Third, I have seen that people are de-formed by the world's informers at such a high rate that the worldview informers have no chance. If we do not realize that television, video games, and the Internet are major danger areas for adverse worldview formation, we are deceiving ourselves. Because these activities take up a larger part of people's lives than meditation, prayer, Bible reading, community, and other such things, we fail to ever come to see the world in kingdom terms.

Fourth, which builds on the last point, is that (more often than not) the people I talk with about this have simply taken secular desires and transplanted them over to Christianity. Most Christians I have met have traded in the good times of secular life for the good times of Christian worship, charismatic teaching, and religious experience. Most Christian college guys I have met have the same worldview as secular guys when it comes to the good life—they still believe that having Jessica Simpson, a band, and airtime on MTV would be the high point of personal existence. They think that calling themselves "Christians" and doing "church stuff" somehow makes their life "Christian," which fails to take Jesus and his mission seriously.

Fifth, people who study hard what they should believe often end up being the most disenfranchised. I have a friend who was a counselor for a seminary, and she told me that her training in counseling was useless for those people because their problems had to do with the fact that they had no idea who they were. Their problem was that they did not know what they believed (only what they *should* believe), and they only *thought* they saw themselves as children of God, but in reality they didn't even know what that meant.

We have already seen that Jesus took the disciples' views of the kingdom and flipped them upside down; we shouldn't expect anything less for us. The disciples' advantage was that they had Jesus standing in front of them saying things like, "Get behind me, Satan!" while we may fail to hear the soft whisper of the Spirit in our own lives. Like Peter, we can easily fail to understand that rebuke and worldview deconstruction are a central part of our existence. We are disciplined because we are loved (Heb. 12:6–11), and we need to have a view of the Christian life that takes this into account.

A Journey of Dependence

It is important that we recognize these aspects of ourselves in the context of Christ's love for us, because the truth about ourselves can be so overwhelming that it provokes sorrow instead of reliance upon grace. Jesus knows what you believe—what you *truly* believe—so it doesn't help pretending it isn't true. It will not help to try and live against the truth of what you really believe—doing so is called "self-help," and is not the "Spirit-help" we find in the Bible. Our goal is not to "get better" but to learn to walk in a journey of dependence upon the Spirit.

When I realized that my lack of prayer said something about what I believed and how I saw the world, I started praying a lot. I started a whole prayer ministry out of it. But what was I really doing? I was trying to make up for my misconstrued worldview by pretending I didn't see the world that way; I tried to bear fruit by force, and yet I remained a sick tree.

Sadly, those around me saw a person who was on fire for prayer, and that meant people followed. Unfortunately, one of the hardest places to look honestly at oneself is in a leadership position; it is far too easy to just act out virtue rather than actually living out of a life with the Spirit. Fortunately, I am not very good at pretending, and because the ministry was built on me and not God, it fell apart.

Looking back, I realize that I wanted to be able to fix my whole prayer issue by myself. I just wanted to affirm the sentence, "I believe that prayer works," and go on my merry way. I wanted to be a self-made man who pulled himself up by his bootstraps and became a man of prayer. Unfortunately, I was still looking at the world from the view of man, not of God. In God's order the process of becoming is often more important than the ideal end[16] In God's order, it seems that the journey must take precedence over the ideal.

It is also important to keep in mind that following Jesus is a way of life, which means that all things (from doing the dishes to prayer) fall under the broader category of discipleship. Jesus is teaching us and will continue to do so through his Spirit. Our task is to be learners of Jesus in every aspect and area of life, and the first step as disciples is worldview development.

I like to think of this in terms of my marriage, but any relationship will serve to make the point. Relationships often grow out of their lowest points. It is after the hard talks or the fights, and even after walking through deaths, depression, or just hard times together that the relationship grows deeper. The same thing is often true in our relationship with God.

One of our greatest struggles will be to open ourselves up to God during these hard times, see the difference between his way and our own, and not shut down. This is the lesson we must learn as God's children from John 6:66–71. The faithful ones do not necessarily get what is going on, but they understand an essential truth about Jesus and about themselves: that only his words have eternal life, while theirs do not.

It is essential for worldview development that we recognize that our life with Christ is not about climbing the spiritual ladder but instead is about walking in intimacy. As we think about growth, we should not think of a continual progression, but a cyclical one.[17] The aim of the Christian life is not independence, but greater dependence; it is intimacy and love, rather than accomplishment and development. Seeing the Christian life correctly is often much more important than we realize. Few have put it as well as Thomas Green, SJ:

> It is not sufficient that the discerning person be "pious" or devout. God may play a significant role in a person's life, and yet there may be no genuine desire to do his will. In fact, one may be a religious fanatic—obsessed by God, by the glory of God—and merely be wedded to one's own idea of God and God's will. This, of course, is not really desiring the Lord's will. But it is a very dangerous and deceptive counterfeit, which has caused much suffering in the history of religion and in the lives of individuals. To genuinely desire God's will, one must be truly *open* to God, a God who is always mysterious and often surprising and disturbing. . . . All of us—even the best of us—will find that our ideas of God frequently block us from truly experiencing him as he reveals himself.[18]

This, among many other reasons, is why it is important to realize that much more is going on in the human psyche than worldview. The central core of one's being, the heart, is where Jesus is going to offer healing and redemption. But that is both outside the scope of this book and outside the scope of my ability to write. Spiritual formation is a passion of mine, but I am too young a person and a believer to write about those things now. I do, however, think that worldview development is a necessary first step in order to enter the task of spiritual formation in a healthy way.

Growth in intimacy requires submission and honesty, opening up to the reality of who we are, who God is, and what God has promised us. This journey goes well beyond what most have asked for when they converted, but it is the path to which God has called his people. In order to grasp this better, we will look again at the worldview informers and how they help in the development of selfview.

THE BIBLE AND SELFVIEW

When Peter recognized who he was in light of who Jesus was (Luke 5:8), he fell down at Jesus's feet. Likewise, when John saw Jesus in his glory, he fell at his feet as though dead (Rev. 1:17). It seems clear that there is something truly terrifying about seeing Jesus in his glory face-to-face. Although he is love, he is also truth, and it seems that the truth he brings can be petrifying.

When we view the Bible as a worldview informer, we'll eventually find ourselves in a place similar to where the disciples were as they stood in front of Jesus and heard his words to them, and chances are those words will be petrifying to us, too. Human nature causes us to avoid these kinds of situations; our great temptation will be to become sedated and numb when we read the Bible, or else we read into the Word an interpretation that protects our heart. In doing so, we use the Word to hide from God, and we undermine the Bible as a means of selfview reformation.

It is important for the sake of selfview that we do not try to merely learn statements about God but that we actually come to hear Jesus preach to us, question us, and maybe even rebuke us. Instead of just memorizing statements like, "Without Christ I can do nothing" (John 15:5) and "In my weakness I am strong" (2 Cor. 12:10), these statements should lead to a place of meditation and openness to God about how much of ourselves still fails to believe these things. One of our great failures as individuals has been to focus on affirming these statements without ever walking with one another in such a way that we can know if they are piercing each other's hearts and exposing our self-aimed selfviews.

In reading Scripture, we need to see ourselves standing side by side with Peter and John as they are exposed by the reality of Christ, and we need to experience that in our own lives. After much distress, I finally realized that this was the first step in believing that prayer worked. I realized that, in the words of Tozer, "Wrong ideas about God are not only the fountain from which the polluted waters of idolatry flow; they are themselves idolatrous. The idolater simply imagines things about God and acts as if they were true."[19] When we are aimed wrongly, we act wrongly.

Unfortunately, I, like many others, was only overburdened by those whose advice boiled down to "try harder." The issue was not one of trying. The issue was that I didn't see the world I lived in to be the kind of place where I needed to pray. *That* was the root of the problem! The fruit was bad because the root had failed to find water.

I am reminded of the only eye-doctor appointment I have ever had. I have been blessed with perfect vision, unlike any one of my relatives. My mother, who assumes that everyone needs an eye doctor, suggested that I go in for a checkup. During this rather odd experience, the doctor was shining some kind of laser in my eye saying, "Keep your eye open . . . just a little longer . . . keep it open." I, of course, am thinking, *Well stop shooting that laser in there and I will! Are you trying to hurt my vision so that I'll actually need to come to you?* All in all, it was a pretty lousy experience, and I vowed never to go back. In a sense, though, this is the Christian life.

God, as pure light, shines his Word into our hearts, and the darkness of our heart fights against it with everything it has. We protect, hide, and guard against all he wants to reveal.

Our task, then, is to have a lifestyle that promotes openness to God. We can't do this on our own, but through the Spirit, the Bible, and community we can be exposed to the penetrating goodness of God's Word.

In the parable Jesus tells of the sower (Matt. 13:18–23), the Word succeeds or fails to penetrate a person based on the status of his or her heart. That should be a continual, and even daily, weight on our lives. We have the ability to ignore and close our eyes and ears to God, and when left to our own devices, we probably will.

Theologian Anthony Thiselton states:

> In terms of world-view, it may be tempting for Christian thinkers to dismiss the work of the three so-called masters of suspicion, Freud, Marx, and Nietzsche, as incompatible with the claims of Christian theology. But their insistence that the human mind can deceive itself in varieties of ways, often in the interests of individual or of social power, resonates with biblical and theological assertions about the deceitfulness, opaqueness, and duplicity of the human heart.[20]

We must always beware of our unconscious desires to look for what we want to be true, the kind of god we think we can follow, instead of seeking the true, mysterious, and wholly other God. Yet, we must keep this kind of self-suspicion in a careful balance. *We can know about God*, which is why we must know ourselves, so that we can fight against our sinful desire to warp God's Word for our own benefit. In order to maintain a balance when we approach the text, we must remember that, in the words of Thomas Green, "True knowledge of God always goes hand in hand with a painful self-knowledge,"[21] and yet "there is now no condemnation for those who are in Christ Jesus" (Rom. 8:1).

Jesus knows what we really believe about him, and he knows that we just don't buy a lot of what he said. What is infinitely worse, though, is that we pretend to believe but don't act. Until we can honestly face the reality that we do not believe the kingdom of God is, for example, "like a treasure hidden in a field" (Matt. 13:44), we will fail to come before God as we really are.[22] Fortunately, our God is a God of redemption, and he is waiting for us to release our views of him and ourselves that we may be transformed.

THE SPIRIT AND SELFVIEW

In order to truly understand who we are in the depths of our beings and how skewed our view of reality is, we need to listen to the person of God living within us. God, who knows us more than we know ourselves and loves us nevertheless, desires to help us see ourselves and him from a redeemed point of view, and central to that task is the Spirit.

I think the reason we talk about Jesus more than the Spirit is because we think we can control Jesus. Jesus seems stuck in the past, or at least stuck in the pages of the New Testament. When we want to avoid the penetrating word of Christ, we can avoid him in the Bible. Also, much of what Jesus said doesn't seem to apply to us anyway, so we even use that as a way to remove the burden of guilt we may feel. In the words of Thomas Green,

> We have a God who entered our plight with us. In the same way that Christ came to know our frailty, he came to understand our struggle to see things as he does.

Even Jesus himself is much easier for us to accept and venerate today because the world of the Pharisees—the worldly values which he denounced in his own culture—is not really our world. We might react very differently if he were to confront us directly, and challenge our accepted secular values today.

This is really the point we were exploring: What is this "world" which militates against the work of the Spirit of God in our lives? It is the cultural air we breathe, the whole complex of values and attitudes which are not really godly, but which we take for granted until the voice of the good spirit breaks into our lives and forces us to question them.[23]

This "good spirit" is not controllable in any way; it is the living and active person within our hearts and minds. We cannot close a book on the Spirit and merely dismiss him or simply avoid verses that talk about the Spirit; he resides with and within us. Unlike the historical Jesus and the groups with whom he interacted, the Spirit interacts with us directly, working all things out for our good whether or not we know, understand, or see it that way.

But in Jesus we have much more than a God who came down to point fingers and judge, we have the first Spirit-filled man to show us how to live. We have a God who entered our plight with us. In the same way that Christ came to know our frailty, he came to understand our struggle to see things as he does. On seeing his coming suffering, Jesus told his followers,

"My soul is deeply grieved to the point of death; remain here and keep watch." And He went a little beyond them, and fell to the ground and began to pray that if it were possible, the hour might pass Him by. And He was saying, "Abba! Father! All things are possible for You; remove this cup from Me; yet not what I will, but what You will."

Mark 14:34–36

What we see in Jesus is a man who knew who he was and who his Father was. Jesus was able to resist the temptation from Satan (Matt. 4:1–11), because he knew better—sin just didn't make sense according to what he knew to be true about reality.[24] Jesus understood what true reality was and knew intimately the Spirit who was with him. What could Satan tempt a man with who communes with the holy God?

The task of self-examination is an essential part of the Christian life, but it must be done with God, not merely by oneself. As put by Simon Chan, in his book *Spiritual Theology*:

> When we search our hearts, we are actually asking the Holy Spirit, the One who "searches all things, even the deep things of God" (1 Cor. 2:10), to examine us. We read in Jeremiah 17:9 that "the heart is deceitful above all things and beyond cure. Who can understand it?" But the verse immediately following says, "I the Lord search the heart and examine the mind, to reward a man according to his conduct, according to what his deeds deserve." Only God can tell us the exact condition of our heart. Self-examination therefore must always be done *in the presence of God*.[25]

It is inappropriate, therefore, to think of *self-examination* as meaning that the *self* is doing the examining; instead, it is the Holy Spirit and you investigating the depths of your heart together. That is why it is so important to look honestly at what kind of theology you live, so that you can be open to the

> The Spirit does not leave us even though he knows the depths of our confusion, our misunderstandings, and our struggle against his view of the world.

Spirit about it. This brings about an interesting dilemma: "We need to examine ourselves in order to pray better, and yet we cannot engage in proper self-examination unless we are in prayer."[26] Our choice is not one or the other but a mutual interaction that will provide a great depth of both.

In the task of worldview development, it is essential that we have a soft heart so that we may hear the word of God as well as the word of the Spirit in our hearts. However, there is always a way for us to foil the Spirit when left to our own devices, which is why it is necessary that we do this within a context of community. The danger with selfview is that we may only see ourselves, by ourselves, with ourselves, and fail to meet the Spirit for transformation.

The Spirit does not leave us even though he knows the depths of our confusion, our misunderstandings, and our struggle against his view of the world. In the task of selfview, we are to commune with the Spirit and not seek ourselves. In the words of Thomas Green, "Self-analysis, and even self-knowledge, is not the goal of the interior life for a Christian; knowledge and love of God are the goal."[27] It is for this that we open our beliefs about God, reality, others, and ourselves up to God: that we may know him deeply and therefore serve and honor him.

COMMUNITY AND SELFVIEW

As we have already seen, being in true community is the best way to prevent reading the Bible through our own worldview glasses or foiling the work of the Spirit in our lives. I don't think I can stress enough how important deep, intimate community is for the health of the Christian life. We often think of the two greatest commandments as things to do, namely, love God and love our neighbor; but this is a framework for how to see reality. Loving God is recognition of who he is, and loving our neighbors is recognition of who they are: creations of God whom he loves.

In terms of selfview, it is easy to see why community is so important. There is a good reason why people are going to counseling in droves; we are a people who need to be known. It is also this desire to be known, and to be in a community of people who know us, that has driven much of my generation's trend of moving back to the cities. There are towns across the Midwest that are finally seeing revitalization after several decades of decline because we have a desire to walk to work, walk to the store, and know people along the way. The isolated coves of suburban life seem dead and lifeless, and we want more.

I think it is important, though, not to assume that just because we now *understand* the need for fellowship, we automatically *believe* in community. Given what we've talked about regarding beliefs, you can probably imagine why. There is a lot of talk about community, and about how, if we would just spend more time with one another, we would have community. But that is impossible; no one is built for this kind of community; it is not of this world. Some may enter it more easily than others, but no one will find it easy.

Community of this kind—deep, vulnerable, and convicting—necessitates that we be prepared for the task of honestly handing over our view of reality to others for them to observe. It means that we do more than just be open about our struggles, but that we actually give people authority in our

We like being able to get the guilt-monkey off our backs by confessing our sin, but we want the community to let us go and sin again and not do anything to stop us.

lives to help point us in a different direction. We are often good with honesty but poor with change. We like being able to get the guilt-monkey off our backs by confessing our sin,[28] but we want the community to let us go and sin again and not do anything to stop us.

It is no wonder that churches with younger congregations struggle to find people who will devote themselves to one church, rather than church hop to experience different services. People aren't looking for depth so much as breadth of community. We somehow think that having a lot of people know a few deep things about us is as good as a few people knowing the depths of us. We take community far enough to fill our felt need of loneliness, but beyond that, we are only replaying the failure of our families to foster community in our lives.

We must take the biblical idea of community seriously for the task of worldview/selfview development to truly take place. Our family life needs to be more concerned with the fact that we have an important mission at hand and that there are plenty of us in the body who fail to see the world as Jesus has called us to see it. This necessitates the kind of depth that most are not comfortable going to, which means that we must come to see this not as an "extra" option of the Christian life, but the heart of it.

It is also important to realize that our larger clan needs to understand the task of selfview. Selfview is as real for churches as it is for individuals. In the words of Karl Barth, "We had best attempt to give no other answer than this, that we are those, that the Church is the congregation of those, who know that they are helpless, but that they are helpless in the presence of One who as their Savior and their Lord is greater than they."[29] We must know who we are, even as a church, in light of who God is.

Our task is not revitalizing the church immediately or changing everything in an attempt to find the "right way to do things"; we are on a journey of redemption. A rightly aimed church is much further along than one that is wrongly aimed but bigger, older, or more experienced in doing ministry. We are on a journey of belief formation; opening ourselves to this journey will prove to be a revolution in and of itself.

> The church should not view community as a tool for getting people to do things.

The task of community also includes looking to brothers and sisters who have walked this road before us. I have prayed with Augustine, "Grant, Lord, that I may know myself and that I may know thee,"[30] because he is my older brother in the faith. Likewise, I have lamented with and been challenged by the words of Jonathan Edwards: "When I look into my heart, and take a view of my wickedness, it looks like an abyss infinitely deeper than hell."[31] Our older brothers and sisters in the faith offer us a glimpse of the Christian life that we need to help us navigate the road ahead.

Like the other two informers, community has its possibilities for negative formation, and sadly, community is often the major culprit of this among the three. One need go no further than one's own community to witness this. We tend to turn inward to the people who look, think, and act as we do, only to reinforce narrow thinking, a misconstrued worldview, and oftentimes false beliefs over real ones. Community has the capacity to be the catalyst for real growth, and yet, when it fails to take seriously the Word and the Spirit, it also has the capacity to neglect the growth of the individual.

This is even more dangerous in our day and age, when people are often driven by the desire to fulfill needs through experience. Community can provide the context for people to be moved internally to act or think a certain way, just based on the strength of their feelings alone. The church should not view community as a tool for getting people to do things. This is a great temptation for the pastors of large churches. I attended a megachurch for a while that would remind us weekly how lucky we were to be there. There are few things as powerful as rhetoric after singing in unison with thousands of other people. These times should be used to point people to God and his call for our lives, not as a time to ask for money, volunteers, or a show of appreciation for how great the music was. There is a time for those things, but the temptation is to do them when it will be most beneficial for the functioning of the church rather than for the soul of the individual.

The task of community should be to honor the Christian life by seeing the journeys of our brothers and sisters as part of our own journey. We must not try to understand our own story outside the story of our family, clan, tribe, or people. This is why Paul had no problem being around nonbelievers but had a problem with believers spending time with Christians who were living without repentance and against the values of the family. Their view of reality will alter our own, and their journey will hinder ours from being done well.

Throughout history the task of selfview has been central to the Christian life. Our goal must be to recover this in our own lives and in the lives of our community. The task of selfview opens us up to the struggle of the Pharisee: that even the most virtuous of activities can be done with great pride, arrogance, and sin. With the help of the worldview informers, we will not only open ourselves up to the transforming power of Christ, but we will show the world a way to live that is far beyond their understanding. As put by Jeffrey H. Boyd: "Clearly we are a people whose self-concept is somehow forged between the hammer of subjective experience and the anvil of the Bible. The Spirit renders our sense of ourselves molten, and the warmth of a worshipping community softens and shapes how we understand our lives."[32]

While we cannot just try harder to change our beliefs, we can live out these realities and trust that God will transform our hearts and minds. Our journey for change, therefore, begins, ends, and progresses by our faith in God and *his* power to transform, not our own.

Our formation is the continual process of the Christian life; our becoming is the defining character of our lives. It will not help us or the movement that Christ started to rest in our own understanding. At the same time, we must be gentle both with ourselves and with others.

Part 3

METAmorpha

A New Way of Living

8

WISDOM

The Road of Human Flourishing

As I mentioned in the previous chapter, when I was in high school I wanted to become a professional athlete, and what may be even worse is that I held onto the belief that it was possible. When I tell this to people I get a look that seems to say, "Couldn't you have come up with a better story than that?" As hard as it is to believe now, I was really holding onto the belief that I could make my scrawny, five-foot-ten-inch frame do things it was never designed to do.

Throughout this book I have tried to offer a model for belief formation. So far, this has remained abstract. While it is not my purpose here to play out what this should look like in your life specifically—trying to do so would prove impossible—I do want to turn directly to the ideology that drove the earliest movement of believers.

In high school my problem was that I was buying into a belief about the good life that was totally unfit for who I was and what I was. In doing so, I made two major mistakes. First, I failed to understand what my gifts and role were, and second, I failed to take seriously the fact that Jesus wanted to transform my view of the good life. The bottom line was that when Jesus talked about coming to give us the abundant life (John 10:10), I just didn't believe it.

> The bottom line was that when Jesus talked about coming to give us the abundant life, I just didn't believe it.

In the history of God's people, the way we have always talked about the good life has been in terms of wisdom. This is why wisdom is such an important discussion in the church today. If we are going to travel honestly on the path of belief liberation, then it is important that we consider the role of wisdom in our lives today.

Looking back, I wish now that someone would have pointed out what was certainly obvious to everyone else—*I had no chance of playing professional sports!* In order to journey well, we have to see the rest of the church body as needing our insight into their lives, and we have to see ourselves as blinded to who we are without their insights as well. In Ephesians 4:25 Paul states, "Therefore, laying aside falsehood, speak truth each one of you with his neighbor, for we are members of one another." In order to live well, we need to live in a constant and mutual interaction with others so that we may come to honor the Spirit's work through them for the shaping of our vision. We cannot merely understand the worldview informers on our own; we need to gain wisdom in prioritizing and engaging them through our interaction within the body. As in my case, the first step we must take is personal. Understanding who I truly am requires that I understand myself not only in relationship with God but in relationship to the body of Christ as well. Our journey is done as a people, but individuals must take every step themselves.

What might help to shed light on our situation is an interesting element mentioned in Genesis 3:7. Without much explanation or explication, we are told that, because of Adam and Eve's sin, their "eyes . . . were opened." Now we tend to think of having our eyes opened as being a positive thing—but in a spiritual sense, it's not. Paradoxically, it seems that with their eyes "opened" they could know each other, God, and themselves even *less* than before. It is counterintuitive to think that open eyes can see less, but as is written in Proverbs 14:12, "There is a way which seems right to a man, but its end is the way of death." Their ability to see rightly was broken, and we are now plagued with the same dysfunction. It is from this point that we have been intrinsically drawn to independence, rather than the dependence that God requires. Our natural assumptions about ourselves, God, and the world are skewed and distorted.

Wisdom as a Way of Life

In the biblical tradition and within the people of God specifically, wisdom has always been an emphasis. In fact, five of the Old Testament books—Job, Psalms, Proverbs, Ecclesiastes, and Song of Solomon—are classified as "wisdom literature." As I have talked with Christians throughout the country, I have noticed that we in evangelical Christianity tend to shy away from most of these books of the Bible. For instance, Proverbs seems too "secular" for our taste, and Ecclesiastes seems too pessimistic. The Psalms are often too heartfelt and honest for our comfort level with God, and Job is too depressing to think about. But the wisdom literature is an overview of the way God's world works. All five books come together into a cohesive whole; they are not to be studied separately but as part of the larger story of God's creation. Because of this, it is important to see the role each type of wisdom literature plays so we may understand what living wisely looks like. Failing to take all of these parts of wisdom *as parts of a whole* is like looking at a photo mosaic without a handful of the pictures; the big picture that explains the individual photos won't become clear, and the pieces will fail to be deeply meaningful.

> But the wisdom literature is an overview of the way God's world works.

Proverbs is a good place to start. Proverbs for many seems just like secular wisdom (e.g., the early bird gets the worm), not spiritual wisdom. What makes the Christian proverbial sayings different is that they are not actually individual sayings; they're individual pictures of a holistic proverbial mosaic showing that the Creator God of the universe is still with us, and he is still acting in our midst.[1] This is the larger picture that helps to bring each individual picture of wisdom literature into greater focus and meaning.

The biblical proverbs help us understand how things typically work. They don't claim things will always work a specific way, but they are generalizations of how God's world tends to function. While "the early bird gets the worm" may be a general truth, there are plenty of examples of people who work hard and go beyond their duties in their career who fail regardless. Proverbs point out the way the world tends to work because of the way it is ordered by God. Because of this, the proverbs are the foundation for living within God's order. The first step toward journeying well is understanding that the world was created in a specific way.

In Proverbs 4:10–27 we learn that, according to God's order, living well means when you walk, "your steps will not be impeded" (v. 12), that "the path of the righteous is like the light of dawn, that shines brighter and brighter until the full day" (v. 18), and that keeping the words of wisdom means not letting them depart from one's sight (v. 21). It is not surprising that in this section the reader is told to "let your eyes look directly ahead and let your gaze be fixed straight in front of you. Watch the path of your feet and all your ways will be established" (vv. 25–26). In Proverbs we learn what it means to journey well and what to avoid along the way.

The Psalms come into the picture to explain the world not merely in terms of dos and don'ts, but as a way of life springing from a deep relationship with God. In Proverbs we read that God knows the ways of a man (Prov. 5:21), so it should be seen as the better side of wisdom to pray with David, "Search me, O God, and know my heart; try me and know my anxious thoughts; and see if there be any hurtful way in me, and lead me in the everlasting way" (Ps. 139:23–24). The Psalms help us see that being known intimately by God, which is the result of opening up to God, is the way to life everlasting.

When we get to the book of Job, we learn that, even though we may search for and follow God with all our lives and

> Proverbs point out the way the world tends to work because of the way it is ordered by God.

hearts, bad things may still happen to us. We also learn that there is much going on in the world of which we are totally unaware and that God's understanding and knowledge are so beyond ours that it is much better to trust in his goodness than our own insight.

Likewise, the writer of Ecclesiastes allows us to live vicariously through him, walking down all the wrong paths so that we don't have to. We are given an overview of life that ends back at the proverbial statement that we are to "fear God and keep His commandments" (Eccles. 12:13). Few books offer a more concise and accurate view of reality than Ecclesiastes, and through "the teacher" we are guided and prodded down the path of wisdom (see Eccles. 12:11).[2] Ecclesiastes allows us to walk in the footsteps of the author and see in ourselves the desire to walk down these paths of foolishness and meaninglessness. At the same time though, our excuse of ignorance is taken away because the life of foolishness is revealed to be foolish, and the life of wisdom is once again grounded in fearing God. After Ecclesiastes, we are without excuse; the writer has exposed the mosaic for what it is—the holistic picture has been revealed.

THE WAYS OF THE KINGDOM

Wisdom breaks down the typical contrast between believing and doing because it focuses on adhering to a reality that is true of the world. We are called to a life of learning about the ways of wisdom that we do not adhere to—not to then mimic the externals of wisdom, but to come to see wisely. Because this is so, wisdom literature does not remain solidified in Old Testament books but is a way of seeing the world that is found throughout the entire Bible. Much of Jesus's teaching is the wisdom principles restated and sometimes expanded. The focus of Jesus's teaching was to help people understand the ways of the kingdom. Jesus's teaching brings us into the realm of wisdom; the kingdom order is God's order, and that is the bedrock of wisdom.

In this sense Jesus was the quintessential sage. He was the wise teacher who understood the way the world worked and, therefore, had the path to life within him. A major aspect of Jesus's teaching was about "the way things were," so it is not surprising then that we should find him teaching about the kind of life that is blessed (Matthew 5). Likewise, in the Old Testament, it is the person who finds wisdom and who gains understanding who is blessed (Prov. 3:13).[3] Jesus then takes these principles and teaches about living the blessed life now—wisdom sayings about the way his kingdom is, and what the good life in the kingdom looks like.

Likewise, we are told that wisdom is better than gold and more precious than jewels (Prov. 3:14–15), that wisdom is a tree of life to those who take hold of her (Prov. 3:18), and on the other hand that the kingdom is like a treasure in a field (Matt. 13:44), and that Jesus is the vine and we find life by abiding in him (John 15:4–5). Wisdom enacted is the kingdom life, and living wisely is living in dependence upon God, knowing that without him we can do nothing.

The *metamorpha* life is a life of wisdom. The key to this life is not merely knowing what the wise life looks like, but coming into the kind of relationship with God that allows us to walk according to the ways of the kingdom. It is in this sense that we are to have kingdom sight, where we *actually*

> The focus of Jesus's teaching was to help people understand the ways of the kingdom.

believe that wisdom is more precious than jewels because that is the way we have come to see the world, and not just a kingdom ideal, where we tell ourselves what the kingdom should be and try to mimic it in our own power.

Jesus's teachings then offer us an acid test for our vision of life. We read his Word and come to see if we have a kingdom way of seeing reality or if we are seeing reality through our own desires and presuppositions. In Jesus's kingdom, we are to test ourselves before we critique our brothers (Luke 6:41–42), we are to count the cost before we follow Jesus (Luke 14:28–33), and we are to, above all else, love God and love our neighbor (Matt. 22:36–40). These are statements about what it means to live the good life, and we should compare them with what we really believe. Are we the people who fail to see the log in our own eye but see the speck in our brother's eye all too clearly? Are we the people who started following Jesus without ever asking if it was going to cost anything? Are we the people who follow God without caring about loving him or our neighbor? Are we living wisely, or are we living as fools?

In Proverbs we have a comparison of wise living and foolish living, which shows the ways of the wicked are not only evil, but they are shortsighted.[4] To live wisely in the new covenant—to live the kingdom life—is to live with vision that is being enhanced by the work of God through the informers rather than having our sight increasingly dimmed by our flesh and the world.

The kingdom is a place where wisdom reigns, where justice and righteousness prevail, and yet it is brought about by the Spirit and not by seeking those things for their own ends. Our mistake has always been to try and *make the kingdom happen* on our own instead of engaging the kingdom reality. Trying to make the kingdom happen is like trying to live out the proverbs without God; good things may happen, and life may work better, but it will fail to be "living wisely" unless it is empowered by the Spirit.

I can remember how, in elementary school, I was trying to find some kind of personality to attach to. I knew, somewhere along the line, I wanted to be a wise person. I didn't use this language, but I understood the concept all the same. In my mind I eventually tied together the idea of sounding smart with being wise, so my solution was to just sound smart.

In conversation with other children I would use abnormally large words, even though I had no idea what they meant. I may have even made up words, knowing that others would probably not call my bluff. The other children started coming to me for advice and assuming that when they had a question I would have an answer—which, of course, I always did. I was playing wise without ever realizing what implications it may have later.

I always knew that my "wisdom" was a farce. I might have fooled others, but I never ceased to feel ignorant, uninformed, and confused. My solution led to my being seen as intelligent, but it didn't change me or the way I lived. I was trying to pretend my way into being wise. While that may seem typical for a child, we do it with holiness all the time. In terms of kingdom living, much more often than not our solution has been to look like we are part of the kingdom without trying to become so.

Later in life I came to realize I could say wise things but fail to be wise. One piece of wisdom that I spouted often but failed to fully grasp myself was, "You reap what you sow." When it finally sank in, it wasn't from reading Galatians 6:7 but from seeing other people's foolishness and realizing that I lived foolishly as well. For some odd reason I thought I could lead out of my own abilities, while failing to take seriously the fact that my life was in disarray. I put on a good show and people followed, but under it all was brokenness.

Fortunately, God has thwarted my attempts to function this way long-term; he has allowed most of my folly to be reaped earlier rather than later. Others are not so lucky. I see people fighting to grow a church in size rather than depth, using their personalities as the driving force behind the growth and failing to take seriously the assumptions and presuppositions they have concerning God. I see leaders preaching well but failing to hold their own families together, and I see their churches, which appear beautiful on the outside like white-washed tombs but are really ugly within, full of dead men's bones as Jesus would say (see Matt. 23:27).

The saddest part of all this is that the church has claimed these vices to be virtues, and we have praised those who live this way. How long before pastors realize that it doesn't help the church to kill themselves in the process of trying to hold things together? When will people learn that family and relationships outlast any kind of work or success? When will we come to truly believe that what we sow, we will then reap?

Jesus embodied kingdom wisdom when he walked the earth, and his call for us is to embody the same kind of wisdom, living by the power of the Spirit. In light of this, we can see the beauty of Jesus's mission. His wisdom kept him dependent upon God, even when God's way seemed too hard to handle (Matt. 26:37–46). Jesus came that our sight might be made new so that we might see rightly. Jesus is the image of the invisible God (Col. 1:15), and because

I put on a good show and people followed, but under it all was brokenness.

of this, Jesus is our lens of God-view. In Jesus we find the mystery of God wrapped up in human form, the wisdom of God not in law or proposition but in flesh. Instead of teaching about mercy, God came and was merciful; instead of demanding faith-fulness, God showed himself faithful. Jesus knew who he was, and he knew how to live a life that was constantly being developed with a kingdom focus, rather than a worldly one. Our call is the same. In order to do this, we need to have wisdom, and we need to function accord-ing to the way God designed reality—with ever-increasing kingdom sight.

> Jesus is our lens of God-view.

PROPER FUNCTION AND SELFVIEW

As a way to talk about living wisely, I'm going to use the phrase "proper function." This phrase carries with it the idea that we and the world around us were made in specific ways. Proper function is the idea that there is such a thing as human flourishing, and God created us with a certain way of life in mind. In this sense, we can talk about health in our spirituality; health implies a way things should be—a way we are to function. Since this is so, let's look now at proper function in relation to selfview and worldview formation. We'll start by looking at proper function in relation to self-view because we must always begin with ourselves and God, and from there start the journey we are to take.

The main issue when we look at proper function and selfview is the concept of "the fear of the Lord"; this refers to confidence in, our commitment to, and knowledge of the

Lord[5] and, in this sense, is the fruit of a spiritually healthy person. Knowing this may help us better understand passages like "the fear of the LORD is the beginning of wisdom" (Prov. 9:10). A healthy fear of the Lord involves understanding who God really is and who we really are, and therefore it rests upon selfview; it is the underlying idea behind the wisdom literature and therefore is central to the discussion of our vision for living. The woman who fears the Lord in Proverbs is said to be wise, Job is described as one who fears God (Job 1:1, 8; 2:3);[6] and we have already seen how Ecclesiastes ends: with a call to fear God and keep his commandments as the underlying guarantee for living well. The fear of God stems from an understanding of God and, more importantly, depends upon a relationship with him. Fearing God is like being stared down by a tiger in the zoo. You are not afraid of the tiger because it is caged, but there is a healthy awe of it *because of what it is*. However, with God we find ourselves confronted with a person who is not caged, and because his power, holiness, and love are unrestrained, we fear him all the more—we stand in awe of him.

The road of wisdom starts with a step of dependence, not one of autonomy. Like the first sin against God, our folly always begins by following our understanding of the world before God's. Jesus called his followers to count the cost because the way he walked demanded a deconstruction and then a reconstruction of one's entire way of seeing reality. The first step is to recognize that one needs saving and therefore needs a Savior, but this process continues on in every area of life.

The posture of dependence requires the willingness to walk through situations we do not understand (e.g., Job), that we do not like (e.g., Jesus in the Garden of Gethsemane), or that we may not have prepared for. One of the most respected Christian spiritualists in our history, John of the Cross, notes that most beginners of the spiritual journey fail to follow God but instead walk their own path. He says, "Many of these beginners want God to desire what they want, and they become sad if they have to desire God's will. They feel an aversion toward adapting their will to God's."[7] The great tragedy of the Christian life is that we can *do* all sorts of Christian stuff and not realize that we have been walking our own path instead of God's.

To live the abundant life Jesus offered is to fix our eyes on the way of wisdom and on Jesus, who has led the way before us by embodying what it means to live according to the reality God created. Wisdom helps us to understand the proverb that Jesus spoke, "Where your treasure is, there your heart will be also" (Matt. 6:21), understanding that it has less to do with finding one's treasure and more to do with finding one's heart. We can't really know what we treasure until we see the depths of our heart—our own treasure room. The wise man values God's way of life, the good and abundant life, and recognizes that one's personal understanding of the good life is warped, twisted, and sad. According to Daniel J. Estes, "The curriculum of wisdom focuses on life, for in observing life the student can become adept at recognizing how . . . [God] constructed his world. In discerning this wisdom, the individual is equipped to function successfully in life."[8] The only sacred and secular split that we find in reality is from the viewpoint of the perceiver. Everything is God's, and people either live toward that end or against it.

In the words of C. S. Lewis, "All our merely natural activities will be accepted, if they are offered to God, even the humblest, and all of them, even the noblest, will be sinful if they are not."[9] C. S. Lewis, in the same writing, also discusses the fact that we may be called to lose our life for the sake of something good, a duty we have as Christians, or even as humans; but we may not be asked to give our lives to anything but God himself. A Christian woman will find herself doing most of the same things a nonbelieving woman would, but the Christian woman needs to do those things according to the will of God, in recognition of the Word of God, and in light of the grace of God. What we do in life won't change as much as the reality of the kingdom in which we live and the reason for why we act in the first place.

> What we do in life won't change as much as the reality of the kingdom in which we live and the reason for why we act in the first place.

In the abundant life, and therefore in the wise life, it is important that we understand that even in the mundane we are constantly being either de-formed or re-formed—we can't stop it. We are either de-formed into the image of the world and our flesh or re-formed into the image of the invisible God. Being wise deals with our individual place in life, our heart, and our relationships—all that need to be informed with kingdom values rather than worldly ones. This is why church programs are anemic. Churches often sacrifice what they should be doing (helping people to live in a kingdom way) for what they've always done (herd crowds of people to do good "Christian" things like volunteer, give, etc.). In the end, people rarely learn the way that God has created his kingdom to be and instead settle for living out their own ideal.

Living with God is a journey into love and not an end; we must journey into this love as learners ready to grow.

Wisdom is subjective because following God is not about doing external things but acting out of a personal reality that we live based on faith and knowledge of God. Our context is important because we have been called to live the gospel in our place and time. We are to learn to love God with all our beings in the time and place in which we find ourselves, and we are to do so with all of our experiences, our pasts, and our hearts.

> Living with God is a journey into love, and not an end; we must journey into this love as learners ready to grow.

PROPER FUNCTION AND WORLDVIEW FORMATION

The task of wisdom is to live in such a way that we are coming to be wise people—people who see the world in a kingdom way. Edward Curtis says, "The wise person must become a craftsman who is able to know how to respond wisely and effectively to any situation that might confront him."[10] Our coming to respond to these situations does not stem from our natural ability to discern but from having our vision of life transformed by God so that we have spiritual discernment. Our goal is to not be overcome with so many voices that we can't actually make a decision but to constantly be in the reality of who God is, who we are, what the kingdom life is, and what we are doing here in the first place.

In order to take seriously the nature of proper function (which stems from wise living) and worldview formation, it is important to look at the nature of wisdom. Wisdom won't fit easily into a box; it will be messy, have ambiguity, and buck against our desire for simplicity and concreteness in life. In many ways, though, this is the nature of Jesus, who always failed to be fit into preconceived boxes and categories. Jesus, as the wise one we are to follow, breaks down all our notions of wisdom and abundant life—but does so out of his knowledge of life and what the abundant life actually does look like.

As we've discussed before, our problem with much of God's reality is that God seems to be more interested in our process than in our arrival (hence our process of transformation). Likewise, God is often more interested in us knowing a little and trusting a lot than in us knowing a lot and having to trust him only a little. This is a sad reality for many who are more academic in nature, who seek to create a system of categories that explain everything God has done, does, and will do. We create a box to put God in and spend the rest of our lives meditating on how impressive a box it is.

> We create a box to put God in and spend the rest of our lives meditating on how impressive a box it is.

The task of wisdom and proper function is much more practical and messy than merely meditating upon God's qualities. Proverbs 26:4–5 helps to illustrate this point: "Answer not a fool according to his folly, lest you be like him yourself. . . . Answer a fool according to his folly, lest he be wise in his own eyes."[11] We are offered two contradicting propositions side by side, both of which are to guide us to live well. For our sake, the Bible refrains from giving us a to-do list; instead, we are offered possible scenarios from which we have to decide the wise path. Wisdom needs to be walked and not merely meditated on. In the new covenant, we walk in and with wisdom now that we have the Spirit residing within us.

Since we are functioning according to God's order and not our own, we need to be prepared to encounter indecision and uncertainty. There will be times when we have no idea what the "wisest" thing to do is. There will be times when we have to walk the delicate balance between knowledge and mystery, between pragmatism and idealism, between truth and love—and in those times it will rarely be clear what the answer is. Yet this is the reality for which we are groomed to live by the worldview informers talked about thus far.

The desire for simplicity and concreteness could be the reason why many stay away from the wisdom literature; we just don't like the fact that it pushes us beyond the text. We want all the answers clearly spelled out for us; we just want to be told what to do. In fact, many people try to make the whole Bible into this kind of Magic 8-Ball, which it was never meant to be. The wisdom literature helps us understand that the Bible is not read within a lab but is read while on the journey—with the Spirit and with other people. Wisdom is required because we have to discern—and we discern because it is more important that we learn dependence upon the Spirit than that we come to the right answers. In the words of Derek Kidner, "The search [for wisdom], strenuous as it must be, is not unguided. Its starting point is revelation . . . ; its method is not one of free speculation, but of treasuring and exploring received teachings so as to penetrate to their principles . . . ; and its goal, far from being academic, is spiritual."[12] We are not left on our own; we are left with God's Word, the Spirit, and the community to help us discern.

I wrote earlier about how the fear of God is the beginning of wisdom and also selfview. This is usually the point at

> The wisdom literature helps us understand that the Bible is not read within a lab but is read while on the journey—with the Spirit and with other people.

which someone experiences conversion—when they realize, possibly for the first time, who they really are and who God really is. They grasp for grace because they are in need. This is the first step of discernment.

My wife's conversion is a good illustration of this. Kelli and her best friend became Christians in college, and they did so because of the community of Christian women who walked beside them. In community with these women, they began to explore the Bible, talk with them about what they were learning, and ask them questions. After a while, Kelli came to a point where she just broke down and knew that she needed God—not so much because God's existence was proven to her but because she couldn't deny that she was missing out on something these other women had.

The unfolding of these events illustrates how naturally, and often obliviously, we use the worldview informers. Kelli was reading the Bible and being guided by it. The community that surrounded her offered wisdom and guidance as she navigated the Scriptures as well as her own soul. The Spirit, known or not, was working within her heart and the hearts of her friends, readying her to hear truths, and speaking those truths directly to her as well.

In all of this, Kelli had to practice discernment. We all had to do this upon conversion. We all come to a point where either our hearts are softened toward God or they are hardened toward him. Sadly, after conversion we rarely enter into the kind of developmental journey we took in conversion. Now that we are "in," we usually just go through the motions of Christianity.

The kingdom life is a developmental journey, and there is no value in just going through the motions. We might not always have the perfect community, and we might struggle to hear the Spirit or to understand the text, but God is constantly working within us as we journey with him through life. God might not make any sense, he might feel distant and out of touch, but we can know, through the testimony of the Bible and our community, that he is completing his good work in us (Phil. 1:6). Our kingdom task, then, is to utilize the worldview informers so we may open up to the work God is doing.

As I mentioned earlier, I became aware of who I was in the order of God and what my downfalls and blind spots were, in light of that new awareness. Likewise, I need to know these same types of blind spots I have with the worldview informers. I need to know if I have the tendency to misunderstand the Bible or read my own interests into it or if I tend to ignore it entirely. I need to understand the role community plays in my life—if it does at all—and what role I play in other people's lives. I also need to examine whether the people around me are trustworthy sources and find out how well they interact with the worldview informers. I need to know from the Bible that the Spirit is working in the depths of my heart, and I need to open up to and submit to his work.

While this may seem overwhelming, we make these kinds of choices and decisions every day—we just don't talk about them like this. We ignore our friend's opinion about something because we question his or her insight. We pray in certain ways because we think that praying "rightly" will somehow spur the Spirit to work, or possibly even more often, we fail to even listen because we assume that the Spirit has nothing to say. Our life speaks volumes about the way we see things, and the way we journey flows directly out of those things.

A Life of Growth

I recall the time when my father realized that he should not remain in the specific kind of church leadership that he was placed in. In his own words, "It was just as freeing realizing what role I was not gifted for in the body as realizing the role I was gifted for." For many, this freedom remains elusive, because the church has forced many into roles and scenarios they were never meant to handle. In our quest to be the body of Christ, we must seek to open up to the reality that we need to have our vision of our own role constantly informed by God and God's people, and that maybe we are not in the position or place we should be. A life of growth will necessarily be a life of formation, and in being formed and guided by the various informers in our life, we will find ourselves more effective for the kingdom.

> In all things, we must not seek to live above or beyond this world, but to understand that we are to live kingdom lives within it.

In all things, we must not seek to live above or beyond this world, but to understand that we are to live kingdom lives within it. According to Gordon Fee, "The purpose of the Spirit's coming was not to transport one above the present age, but to empower one to live within it."[13] We are given power that we may live the kind of life that Jesus would live if he was in our place—and that should serve to be one of the most awe-inspiring ideas we will ever meditate upon.[14]

We are in an age, unlike the earliest believers, where we can function reasonably well, even in Christian circles, without any of the worldview informers having a significant influence in our lives. It is easy to be a Christian in our culture, and our livelihood does not depend on our growth and dependence upon God and the community of believers. On the opposite end of the extreme, the earliest Christians were constantly reminded of how desperate their situation was because of persecution, poverty, disease, war, and so forth. Christians in many other parts of the world still continue to live this way. But that is not, for whatever reason, the situation most of us are faced with. The point is not to feel guilty because of our freedom but to live the kingdom where we are and wherever God leads us. But in light of that, we need to keep in mind that *we are not faced with persecutions, and it is often persecution that helps to keep the kingdom reality clear for us.* Persecution helps to force the issue of dependence upon the Christian, while freedom usually allows Christians to depend on themselves and their own ability instead of on God's. We need to recognize how easily we function without even thinking about God, his Word, and each other, and we need to make sure our lives are set up in such a way to force us to consider these things.

I had a project in seminary where I had to read through all of Paul's letters several times and write a paper on one of the themes I identified. I figured that I should try to work on something I wasn't familiar with, so while I was reading I tried to be more aware of ideas or language that I might normally pass over. What I saw amazed me. Paul had a constant understanding of the possibility that the world he was in could be near its end, and he understood his work and his role within that reality to be hugely important. I, on the other hand, had no such clarity, either about the world or about myself.

This study led me to consider my worldview and to turn to the Spirit to confess that I never think about judgment, death, and Christ's return, and that most of the people I run into who dwell on the end times kind of scare me. It made me realize how often we as Christians ignore major themes of Scripture just because of what one group, or even one person, might do with that theme. Yet how many of us allow what other extremists believe to affect what we do and permit our growth to be hindered because of it? Just as I had to come to grips

We have to
choose wisdom,
even if it puts us
in a camp with
those from whom
we would like to
separate ourselves.

with my own blind spots, regardless of what others believe, we have to choose wisdom, even if it puts us in a camp with those from whom we would like to separate ourselves.

Living wisely, as we have seen, is much more than merely following certain rules of life, although that does have a part; it is a lifelong journey with the worldview informers guiding our sight, our path, and our aim. The Bible, the Spirit, and our community act as the root system of a tree planted by streams of water, which takes in abundantly and nourishes the tree so that it will function properly.

We are told in Proverbs 10:17 that "he is on the path of life who heeds instruction," pointing to the fact that the wise person is forever teachable. The path of the wise man will never be his own but will constantly be informed by the reality that God has put him in, the text that God has given him, the Spirit that lives within him, and the travelers along the way with him.

Wisdom is living well, but it is more than that: it is living in dependence. Old Testament theologian Lawrence Toombs wrote, "It appears that the search for wisdom, demanding as it is, does not lead directly to wisdom, but to God. . . . The result of the search for wisdom is that strange admixture of love and awe . . . which the Old Testament knows as the 'fear of the Lord.' The end of the quest is also that intimate personal fellowship with the Eternal which is the 'knowledge of God.' "[15] Living well is living wisely, and it is in this life that we find communion with God: resting in his perfect will, his peace, and his understanding rather than our own.

9

THE WAY OF JESUS

Life through Death

Bill spent the day with a class of elementary school children while they were on a field trip. It had been an uneventful day, and he'd spent most of the trip flirting with the teacher. But as the teacher was rounding up the children at the end of the day, he noticed a child who was standing facing a wall. Bill approached the child and saw that he had wet his pants. He was faced with the options of either helping the child or letting him fend for himself. Bill made an unusual choice.

Seeing a nearby water pump, Bill took water and made it look like he too had wet his pants. Instead of throwing water on the child to make it look as if it wasn't urine but water, Bill decided the best option was to enter into the child's humiliation with him.[1]

As odd as Bill's decision might seem, his actions embodied the reality of the incarnation. God heard the cries of his people, and his solution was to enter into our pain and humiliation—to save us from within our suffering.

I can't fathom what it was like to be one of the earliest disciples. Their response to Jesus was a lot like mine was to Bill: *There has to be a better plan that this!* Jesus was nothing like what they expected, and he was everything they weren't looking for. As one theologian friend of mine has said in reference to how drastic the disciples' worldview deconstruction would have been, "There has not been a greater paradigm shift in all of history as the one the disciples had to endure."

Up until now our discussion has focused on the worldview informers. Now we're going to turn our attention to Jesus and the life he lived. The way of Jesus is living according to the kingdom life now—as we were meant to live it. Jesus's life, death, and resurrection ushered in an age when people were inwardly empowered to live according to the wisdom of God. Jesus preached that the kingdom was now here, and his life was the embodiment of kingdom values. Jesus walked the way he did because he saw the unseen kingdom, and likewise our call to see rightly includes this new kind of vision: kingdom seeing.

KINGDOM SEEING

At one point in Jesus's ministry, a group of Jewish elders came to him to ask a favor (Luke 7). A friend of theirs, a Roman officer, needed Jesus to heal his servant.

I'm sure that these kinds of scenarios were typical for Jesus. Going from town to town healing people would make you a pretty popular person. This story could be read as if it were *just another* healing story in the ministry of Jesus. Even though healing stories are always amazing, they soon lose their individuality.

In the end Jesus heals the servant, which is not surprising, even to those who are following him. They have probably seen Jesus heal many people. Even more amazing is Jesus's proclamation about this Roman centurion, whom he had never actually met. Jesus exclaimed, "Not even in Israel have I found such great faith" (Luke 7:9). Jesus saw a man walking according to the reality of the kingdom, and he was amazed.

It is easy for us to talk about the present kingdom of God, because we understand it to be a spiritual reality that we have access to and that is working within us. But it would have been beyond strange for a scribe to hear from Jesus that they are not far from the kingdom (Mark 12:34) or for a Pharisee to hear that they will not be able to point to the kingdom and say, "Here it is!" or "There it is!" and that it was actually in their midst (Luke 17:21). Few things would have been as counterintuitive and backwards in their minds as this. It just wouldn't have made sense.

That is why this Roman officer's faith is so amazing. The officer seemed to see what no one up to that point had been able to see: Jesus was a king, but not one ruling just over people but over sickness as well. It took someone outside of the Jewish worldview to understand Jesus had this kind of power. Being an officer, the Roman understood what it meant to be under authority. He would have been familiar with receiving assignments from those above him in the name of Caesar. This man understood how kingdoms work; he was a part of a very large earthly kingdom. Amazingly, he saw these same principles at work in Jesus and believed that the sick could be healed in the name of Jesus.[2]

The officer may have understood the nature of Jesus's gospel message more than anyone else up to that point. He saw a kingdom at work in the way of Jesus that was not restricted by natural boundaries or dependent upon physical realities, and it was of such authority that he could speak sickness away. It was in this sense that the officer saw in Jesus the unseen reign of God; he saw the kingdom of God.

The Jewish expectation was for the Messiah to have God with him, which is how he would accomplish all of the tasks he was to carry out. In doing so the Messiah would usher in the kingdom of God. Jesus, on the other hand, claimed that the kingdom was already here and that individuals must enter into it to be with God. His explanation of following God had nothing to do with ethnic or national boundaries but with a common relationship believers have with God that grounds their identity as his children.

In light of this, a relationship with God is exactly what Jesus offered, but he did so through himself. Jesus was and is the door that must be walked through for entrance to the kingdom, which means that his way must be walked for access to the abundant life. Entrance to the kingdom was made possible because Jesus, the personification of wisdom, is *the* way of life—where wisdom and kingdom theology intersect. Wisdom offers a framework for the way things are and the way things work. The kingdom offers the counterintuitive claim that the first will be last, the weak strong, and the dead made alive.

Therefore, until we can make sense of the fact that Jesus is the King who came to serve, the God who came to die, and the Judge who came to reconcile, we will not be able to see the kingdom reality. It is this reality that was, and continues to be, a stumbling block for so many. The way of Jesus is a submission to the backwards way of God. We must come to see the world as Jesus did, as a place where the way of power is through weakness, the way of life is through death, and the way of love is through the cross.

LIFE THROUGH DEATH

We all assume an image of God in our minds, whether he is angry, merciful, full of wrath, or full of love. It would have been no different for Paul. As Paul journeyed to Damascus doing what he thought was the work of his God, he was met by Jesus in a great light from heaven. It is probably impossible to fully appreciate the intensity of this experience, not only in seeing a light from heaven and meeting Jesus himself, but in the realization that the work you have devoted to God has led you to fight against him.

For the next three days, Paul experienced physically how God saw him spiritually: blind and in total darkness. What we have in Paul's experience is an archetype of all our experiences. While they will each differ in detail, all our experiences carry traits of Paul stumbling over God's reality as he was journeying to fulfill his own.

After three days of darkness, Paul could see once again. While we have no idea what Paul was thinking, it is certain that much of this time was spent meditating on the fact that Jesus is who he proclaimed himself to be, that he, Paul, was working against God, and that somehow the Messiah was crucified and was now reigning with God. He was struck all at once with the reality that everything he had devoted himself to was misguided, and even though he had taken part in the murder of God's own people, he was given grace and allowed to take part in the mission of God.

Paul walked according to his own assumptions, influenced by his own informers. The journey he was on was guided directly by assumptions about Jesus, not by Jesus himself. Like Paul, we must come to understand that sometimes the darkness of our reality allows us to be guided by God. Our ability to journey well will depend on our ability to see the darkness as a gift from God, leading us to and not away from him. This darkness is not absence from God but a way to open our hearts and reality to him.

Paul's view of reality goes through an enormous shift. He had to take the first step of wisdom: getting an adequate knowledge of God and of oneself. From this standpoint, Paul tells two opposite stories about his life prior to knowing Jesus. The first we find in Philippians 3:6, where he states that, as to righteousness, he was blameless under the law. Paul, as a Torah-observant Pharisee, sees his old life as the prime example of religious faithfulness. Yet in Titus 3:3 Paul includes himself when he says, "We ourselves were once foolish, disobedient, led astray, slaves to various passions and pleasures, passing our days in malice and envy, hated by others and hating one another" (ESV). Understanding how these two descriptions coincide is the key to comprehending how Paul understood kingdom values. His life was foolish, not because he did not live well according to the standards of the day, but because he had not yet understood the wisdom of God.

All of his life had been devoted to the Pharisaic tradition. He had not only lived blamelessly in this tradition, he was achieving to a higher degree than many of his contemporaries. But looking back at his life through the lens of the cross, Paul saw something new. He was able to see his heart. Suddenly all of the action, discipline, righteousness, and devotion could be seen for what it really was. Paul had tried to bear fruit through power, but now he understood how the cross calls us to bear fruit through weakness.

For Paul, the cross was the major stumbling block that he calls the "wisdom of God." It is a stumbling block because it is seen as folly by those who are not in the kingdom. After the darkness of Paul's three days of blindness, and after the darkness the disciples felt while Jesus was in the tomb, their new vision was totally reoriented to the cross. Quoting Neil Elliott, New Testament theologian Michael Gorman suggests that "Paul's mission in life was to seek to 'order the lives of Christian congregations by pulling everything into the tremendous gravitational field of the cross.' . . . *The cross is the interpretive . . . lens through which God is seen; it is the means of grace by which God is known.*"[3]

The entire story Paul lived by was reoriented around the fact that God had come to earth to give himself out of love. It is within this narrative that we need to read Paul's statement in 1 Corinthians 2:2: "I determined to know nothing among you except Jesus Christ, and Him crucified." It was within this understanding of the world that Paul could preach with kingdom power. It was not of himself, but of God's willingness to put on human weakness.

Two Résumés

It is in light of this that Paul gives his rather impressive résumé in Philippians 3 and ends it by saying, "But whatever things were gain to me, those things I have counted as loss for the sake of Christ. More than that, I count all things to be loss in view of the surpassing value of knowing Christ Jesus my Lord, for whom I have suffered the loss of all things, and count them but rubbish so that I may gain Christ" (Phil. 3:7–8). Paul followed the way of Jesus, which is the story of love and so, necessarily, is the story of the cross.[4]

It would be wrong to suppose that the cross was an anomaly in Jesus's life. It was the aim and direction of all of Jesus's life. Likewise, when Paul gives his résumé he actually parallels it with Jesus's "résumé of shame" listed in Philippians 2. Paul's résumé goes up the ladder of success, showing how he is impressive, successful, and different,[5] whereas Jesus's résumé starts at the top (divinity) and ends with the cross:

Philippians 2:5–8 —Jesus's Résumé	Philippians 3:4–6 —Paul's Résumé
Have this attitude in yourselves which was also in Christ Jesus, who,	If anyone else has a mind to put confidence in the flesh, I far more:
• although He existed in the form of God, • did not regard equality with God a thing to be grasped, • but emptied Himself, • taking the form of a bond-servant, • and being made in the likeness of men. • Being found in appearance as a man, • He humbled Himself by becoming obedient to the point of death, • even death on a cross.	• circumcised the eighth day, • of the nation of Israel, • of the tribe of Benjamin, • a Hebrew of Hebrews; • as to the Law, a Pharisee; • as to zeal, a persecutor of the church; • as to the righteousness which is in the Law, found blameless.

Paul can now look back at his résumé and proclaim that he counts it all "as rubbish" only because he has lived through, and now sees the world through, Jesus's résumé. Jesus reoriented power and success around the cross and lived according to this understanding of the world by walking to the cross. The cross was not an anomaly; rather it was the culmination of the kind of life Jesus lived.

Our attitude should mimic that of Jesus, because he lived according to kingdom values. His life was not flippant—it was strategic. We, like Paul, now find ourselves trying to succeed at life in the shadow of the cross. This is why it is important to see that the death of Jesus was more than an untimely end to an impressive ministry; it was the nature of that ministry. The cross was Jesus's aim throughout his life, that he would be the vessel of grace to the world. In the cross we see the God of love as he is, and as he always has been: a God of mercy, grace, and selflessness.

> The cross was not an anomaly; rather it was the culmination of the kind of life Jesus lived.

THE WAY OF THE CROSS

Paul did not see the cross of Christ as merely an event in history or an aspect of his theology that he had to admit happened; the cross represented a revolutionary way of life. The cross held within its symbolism the painful tension between life and death that we presently experience. As death was winning over Christ on the cross, life was being won at the same time. Likewise, death is quite literally working itself out in our bodies, while the Spirit is working inside of us for life.[6]

Similar to this, we can understand the kingdom reality that, while death is winning over the world, life is being birthed and established in the kingdom. Just as the roots of a tree move into greater and greater darkness to help bring about the reality of the branches reaching up toward greater and greater light, it is through the way of darkness that we meet with the Father of light. As God utilizes the worldview informers to work together in our hearts, our minds, and our behavior, we may feel as though it is death working, but it is the work of Christ. Like the disciples and Paul after them, we must live a life of pliability, so the potter can always work with a moldable lump of clay. This is what I mean by a life of *metamorpha*.

Many Christians live a life of frustration and depression because they, like Paul on the road to Damascus, live a life of service to God and do not realize that they are living for what *they believe* God to be like rather than what he *is* like. We all should be on a journey to greater knowing, and that can only be done if we are ready to hear the rebuke from Jesus or to walk though a time of "blindness" with him.[7]

In our postmodern world, there has been a heightened sense of worry about offering a metanarrative—an overarching story in which to frame reality. The assumption is that all metanarratives are oppressive narratives.[8] In Christianity, the metanarrative we find is the way of Jesus, the way of the cross. It is a narrative that liberates through slavery, finds life in death, and puts oneself last to be found first. The way of Jesus is far from oppressive; in fact, it offers the presence and power of the kingdom to all, without prejudice.

For the earliest Christians, the idea of life through death and the way of the cross were intimately connected. Commenting along these lines, New Testament theologian James Dunn states, "*To experience the exalted Christ therefore is to experience not merely new life but new life which is life through death, life out of death, and which always retains that character.* As soon as the exalted Christ is separated from the crucified Jesus, charismatic experience loses its distinctive Christian yardstick."[9] This is the reorientation that must take place. We are given a new yardstick for measuring life in God; we cannot use merely our feelings, experiences, and knowledge as the measure of our maturity.

This yardstick is what Paul refers to when he writes, "Brethren, join in following my example, and observe those who walk according to the pattern you have in us. For many walk, of whom I often told you, and now tell you even weeping, that they are enemies of the cross of Christ" (Phil. 3:17–18). If we accept eternal and abundant life without the crucifixion, we deny the way of Jesus, and likewise if we live like the world does, by building impressive résumés for the kingdom, we will find ourselves at odds with it.

This is why the person who just thinks positively and isn't open to being deconstructed by the Word, the Spirit, and community has a really hard time with the Christian message. It is through and in the reality of facing our sin, and not the reality of what we accomplish, that we come to find release in the Spirit. Those who avoid their sin are like a trio of musicians that refuses a lifeboat and continues playing music while the ship is sinking because they think that reality can be changed by focusing on something more satisfying and palatable.

The way of the cross leads naturally *to* humility and dependence, and *away* from pride and independence. It would be foolish, though, to believe that we can't use the cross for division and pride; we most certainly have and could. But the stance of the Christian is to follow the one who went the way of the cross, the way of humility. Our own strength cannot be used to make the Christian life happen. We must be guided by God as he works in our hearts and our lives. The way of Jesus is submission; it is the way that leads to the cross.

The worldview informers are to help shape our stories so that we follow a crucified Christ and come to have cruciform love. Unfortunately, this is hardly the common understanding of the Christian life. We often talk about "bearing our cross," but we do so without preparing to live through Gethsemane. It is only by the Spirit of God working in our hearts that we can beg God to remove this cup from us, yet end with "Not my will, but yours be done."

> It is only by the Spirit of God working in our hearts that we can beg God to remove this cup from us, yet end with "Not my will, but yours be done."

When Paul wrote to the Corinthians he let the cross speak for itself as the wisdom of God (1 Cor. 1:18–31), proclaimed that the Spirit who searches the depths of God (1 Cor. 2:10) is in our hearts, and added that we now have the mind of Christ (1 Cor. 2:16). The spiritual reality of our lives is that without the Spirit of God within us we could not possibly understand the way of Jesus. It won't make sense. That is why even in our openness to God we must realize that the wisdom of the kingdom is beyond our ability naturally, but it can be ours spiritually.

THE WAY OF FAITH

I recently had a rather odd conversation with my friend Ed that went something like this:

"Kyle, what would it take for you to trust a total stranger?"

"A lot, I imagine," I replied, not understanding where he was taking the conversation.

"Well, what if this stranger's request required nothing from you but had a really good chance for great gain?"

"Well, I suppose I would take the chance, as long as it didn't require much."

"What if it was possible that you could lose a lot, but there was also a great chance for gain," he replied, pushing the conversation further than I wanted it to go.

"I don't know. . . . I probably wouldn't trust him if I had a lot to lose. Why would I; I don't even know him?"

"I imagine, if you are like me, that you wouldn't really trust him until you had no other choice, is that right?"

"Yeah, I guess. Why?"

"I think this is how we treat God. We say we trust him, but it is only for things like salvation, which is out of our hands anyway. What usually ends up happening is that God has to lead us to a place where we have no other choice but to trust him. It is at that place where we learn to have faith. If we don't trust him there, he will continue to bring us there until we do."[10] At this point my friend opened his Bible to Genesis and proceeded to talk about Abraham, the man of faith.

In Genesis 12:1–3 God tells Abraham (then Abram), "Go forth from your country, and from your relatives and from your father's house, to the land which I will show you; and I will make you a great nation, and I will bless you, and make your name great; and so you shall be a blessing; and I will bless those who bless you, and the one who curses you I will curse. And in you all the families of the earth will be blessed." Paul even tells us in Galatians 3:8 that this was the gospel told to Abraham: that through him all the earth would be blessed. In Jesus, we find the fulfillment of that promise.

While there is no doubt that Abraham struggled to know what God meant by all these things, or how they would play out in his life, it is clear that Abraham believed God. He took God seriously and believed that God's promises were worth staking his life on. Because of Abraham's abundant trust, he is called the father of faith, and as children of faith, we are considered his spiritual offspring.

In Hebrews 11 we see the essence of our family resemblance: faith, which "is the assurance of things hoped for, the conviction of things not seen" (v. 1). Abraham believed the story God told him, and he knew that God's ways and promises were far beyond him. Abraham's faith is so prominent because he took a journey into the unknown, without seeing how God's promises made sense, and yet lived according to the reality God promised, not the reality he saw.[11]

For most of his life Abraham lived with the promise of an heir through whom the world would be blessed. But as the years passed and he and his wife, Sarah, got older, he sank into the darkness of doubt and Sarah's barrenness. The light in that darkness—the birth of his son Isaac—was plunged back into darkness when the Lord requested Isaac as an offering. But because of Abraham's willingness to follow the Lord in all things, the light was not snuffed out. Like Paul, Abraham had to walk in darkness with the Lord in order to see the light on the other side.

God's promises to Abraham were answered in small doses, but Abraham had to trust that these small answers would prove God trustworthy for the greater claims he had made about Abraham's descendants. As put by the author of Hebrews, "All these died in faith, without receiving the promises, but having seen them and having welcomed them from a distance, and having confessed that they were strangers and exiles on the earth" (Heb. 11:13). Even as exiles on earth the faithful could live by a hope in something that they would not see within their lifetime. Abraham knew God to be a trustworthy God, and he believed God's promises. He walked, not by what he saw, but by what he knew to be true from the Word of God.

We do not have eyes to see in our natural condition. We journey trusting God's Word about the nature of the kingdom, and the Spirit and the community work in our hearts mirroring back to us the reality of who we are that we may be inwardly empowered to follow God. As has been wisely said, "Those who walk by sight eventually learn that seeing may be misleading."[12] We must utilize a kingdom type of sight that depends on God's way of seeing instead of our own. Fortunately we have those who have walked before us, like Abraham, from whom to learn the way of faith.

I remember hearing all of the horror stories about the tsunami, which destroyed so many people's lives but had not left one animal dead. The news kept on talking about the odd reality that the animals knew something that the humans did not—they had some kind of perception that warned them of the coming danger. In a sense, they had eyes to see that which we as humans do not. Likewise, kingdom sight is a way of perceiving a reality that does not make sense to those who do not have eyes to perceive it. We may be seen as odd for acting upon this sight, but the way of faith is the way into the world that God has created and called us to, and it is from this perspective that we are called to live.

The book of Habakkuk shows faith from a different perspective. Habakkuk understands that God is going to judge his people, and he certainly understands why. What Habakkuk cannot understand for the life of him is why the Lord is going to use a pagan and wicked people to judge his own. It just didn't make sense. *They certainly need more judging than we do, no matter how wicked we have been.* Habakkuk ends his frustrating conversation with the Lord by saying, "Yet I will exult in the LORD, I will rejoice in the God of my salvation. The LORD God is my strength" (Hab. 3:18–19).

Habakkuk does not understand God but remains faithful nevertheless.

Job knew God was righteous and that what was happening to him was evil, but it was his own self-estimation that led him astray. Job thought he could discern the reality of good and evil, and instead he ended up defending his own innocence and demanding an answer from God. Habakkuk, on the other hand, knew what God was doing and knew God to be good, but he still couldn't understand *why* God was doing what he decided to do. Even so, he recognized his ignorance, and he stood on the fact that God is trustworthy and that his ways were far above his own.

> We must confess that it is much easier to rely on our North American pragmatism, our business savvy, or our own personal charisma than to rely solely on God.

What we find in Abraham, Job, and Habakkuk are differing models of faith. Abraham believed God and trusted in his promises for the future, and so he is the father of faith. Job had faith that God was good but also had faith in his own understanding, and so he found himself humbled. Likewise, Habakkuk thought that he understood what *fair* should look like, and was vocal about his concerns, but he ended by focusing on God's way above his own.

In all of these figures, as well as other heroes of faith, we find glimpses of what perfected faith might look like. What we find in Jesus *is* perfected faith—a total trust and abandonment to the way of God. Too often we wait until we have nowhere else to turn before we actually trust God. We find it easy to trust God for our salvation, but after that we live by our own estimation of reality. That is why we need to see the extent to which we follow our way above God's before we can submit to the way of Jesus.

We must confess that it is much easier to rely on our North American pragmatism, our business savvy, or our own personal charisma than to rely solely on God. But when we rely on something other than God, we stray from the path and start heading for the wilderness. It is only when God is the one guiding the process of our growth that we come to journey according to God's order over our own. Interestingly, when the disciples needed several men in Acts 6 to take care of the amount of food handed out to the widows of the region, they did not choose men with mere business acumen. Instead, they looked for men of good reputation, full of the Spirit and of wisdom. They initiated them into their new position by praying for them and laying hands on them. The earliest disciples recognized what we often fail to, that the way of the world does not make sense according to the way of Jesus.

The philosophy of the earliest believers was that every position in the body, no matter how remedial and simplistic it may seem to be, is a deeply spiritual endeavor. They recognized that all activities, whether ministry related or not, are used by God for the benefit of growth, discipline, and opening to who he is. Sadly, our understanding today is often vastly different.

The way of Jesus involves walking a path of deeper intimacy with God. Just as the disciples were guided and developed by Jesus, sometimes with a hard hand and sometimes with a soft touch, Jesus will guide and discipline us. He does so that we may come to see past our own limited vision and learn to love him, know him, and follow him in eternal life. Faith in Jesus is learning to live according to the reality that makes no sense to us naturally but is known as eternal life to those who will follow.

Jesus himself walked the path of light through darkness, taking the way of the cross—the way of faith—as our example. We see him in Gethsemane praying that God would remove the cup he was about to take, but like Habakkuk, he ends by releasing his own will to God's. Jesus acted the way he did, not simply because he knew more than we did, but because his faith was greater than ours.[13] Jesus's faith was grounded in trust of his father; he really believed that God's way was better than man's.

We are called to believe that the reality in which we live is inundated by the love of God and that he is offering a way to live that is far removed from anything else the world has ever seen. The way of Jesus is so different, the Gospel of John says, that we are told that the world will hate us for living it (15:18–25). In that same section of John we are told that in order to bear fruit, we are to abide in Jesus. It is to the act of abiding in Jesus that we now turn.

10

DISCIPLESHIP

At the Foot of the Master

I remember the time in my life when *I knew* I needed to be discipled. Others around me talked about their experiences with a mentor, guide, or sage. Some had been discipled in the past, but many currently sat at the feet of these leaders. Wherever I looked, however, I failed to find someone with the time, energy, or desire to walk by my side.

Most of my prayers on the subject ended up being rants of frustration. *Could there possibly be a good reason why God wouldn't want me to be discipled?* I didn't understand why he wouldn't provide me with someone as a guide but instead would leave me to walk in the dark. It's not that there wasn't anyone around who provided me with guidance and direction; there certainly was. But none of them acted as people in whose steps I could follow. I didn't know how to walk or which way to go, and it seemed as though God wasn't listening.

On the surface of things it seems like discipleship should be one of the easier things to grasp within Christianity. We are, after all, called to "make disciples" of all nations. But rarely have we spelled out what that means, let alone what it should look like. We talk about making converts and getting them involved in programs, small groups, and even mentoring relationships, but we rarely talk about the developmental process of belief transformation.

It is here that we can begin to ask the question "Where is Jesus?" We have talked about Jesus's life as a model of the Christian life, but now we need to turn to Jesus himself. We must not only walk the way of Jesus but also walk *with* Jesus. It is only with and in Jesus that we find the true Christian journey, and our growth as disciples comes from our abiding in him.

WITH JESUS: THE ANCIENT PATH

It is human nature to focus on side issues instead of core issues, temporal things over eternal, and other people rather than Jesus. We are easily drawn to external aspects of the faith we find attractive, whether it be good music, social action, or a dynamic speaker, and expect that to be the answer to all of our problems. It seems that many are looking less for Jesus than for solutions to their felt desires and values. The path we take often says much about the culture we have grown up in, the values we have always held, and the vision we have for what "the good life" should look like. As we previously discussed, the Jesus way of life—the way of the cross—is foolishness to the world.

What we see in the prophets in the Old Testament, as well as in Jesus, is a call to the good life, life with God.

The prophet Jeremiah looked on the people of Israel and saw a nation that had lost its way. Jeremiah encouraged the nation with these words: "Stand by the ways and see and ask for the ancient paths, where the good way is, and walk in it; and you will find rest for your souls" (Jer. 6:16). When Jesus comes on the scene, the good life gets revised; Jesus is now the way, the truth, and the life (John 14:6), and he is the ancient way that Jeremiah alluded to. The Christian life is thus a Jesus way of life; it is walking with him according to the way he walked before us.

> North American Christianity, as I see it, has been made more in the image of what we want to be true than what *might actually be true.*

The idea of journeying and walking with God is one of the classic biblical metaphors for Christian living. Yet phrases like "walking with God" and "Christianity is not a religion, it's a relationship" have become clichés we take for granted but don't really know how to live out. If nothing else, it is clear that all of this talk has amounted to very little change in the church and the way we live as disciples.

North American Christianity, as I see it, has been made more in the image of what we want to be true than what *might actually be true.* Upon conversion, we tend to bring together our ideas, assumptions, and desires, toss in Jesus, and then go on with life. We may convert to a new social group, a new Sunday morning agenda, and a new book club, but rarely do we feel we've been adopted into a new family with a new kingdom and a new story.

With Jesus it is different. In Jesus we find the first human being who walked completely by the Spirit and told his story in the shadow of his Father, determined to walk in the way in which he was called. As we have seen, the way of Jesus is not a program to follow but is instead an ideology that should be driving all of our programs. Jesus did not set in stone the ways we should act; instead, *he gives us a path to journey on with him*. And different people walk different paths of Christian faith. As I have been suggesting, the Christian life is not a fixed path that all must first find and then follow, as if we all started from the same point. We will not live, act, and walk identically.

For the disciples, to talk about "the way" of Jesus was simply to talk about being with Jesus—following him. The way of Jesus can be tried, but if it is done apart from being with him, it will be a failure. Borrowing Eugene Peterson's terminology, we can try to do *Jesus things*, but unless we do them in *Jesus ways*, it will prove fruitless.[1] The fruit in discipleship will come from doing Jesus things in Jesus ways, which stems from a deep and intimate personal relationship with Jesus, as he had with his Father.

Many of us walk around guilt-ridden, not understanding our role in the kingdom and not finding God anywhere. Those of us who have struggled with this usually begin by talking about what the Bible says *should* be true, chastising ourselves for not living that way, and then trying harder to do what is right. This method doesn't work because it is done solely in our own power—without God. It is self-help, which is the way of man, not the way of God. When our struggles take us to guilt and not to God, we walk under the burden of law and not grace. Unfortunately, this attitude reflects the approach most sermons take: they give us information on what we have failed to do and then offer a self-help program to fix it. We do not need more ways to fix ourselves; we need to find ourselves in the love and grace of God, turning to him and his power to change us.

Fortunately, Jesus takes us beyond self-help and calls us instead to a journey of redemption in all areas of life. Jesus opened his arms to the disciples, offering them a new family, a new way of life, and a renewed understanding of God's presence with his people. He offered the crowd an invitation to worldview deconstruction and a life with God, welcoming all who would come and commit to the journey. But Jesus did not send them to a school or a training camp; rather, he entered life with them. Jesus's form of discipleship did not have a specific place or time but took place wherever he was, whether walking, eating, or preaching.

How do we make disciples in light of the ministry of Jesus? As with anything, we tend to make a lot of assumptions about the discipleship process, usually based on our given tradition or experience. If we are going to take seriously our call to make disciples of all nations, it is important that we first understand what it means to make disciples in our place and time. The early Jesus movement was effective because the disciples knew what the disciple-making process entailed.

MAKING DISCIPLES: OUR ROLE

There is a popular preacher I used to listen to. His approach was unusual and his content usually offered something to think about, so I kept up-to-date on whatever sermon series he happened to be going through. Before long, his style, viewpoint, and demeanor were drilled into my consciousness, as often happens after listening to a person teach for lengthy periods of time. During this time a friend asked me to listen to a talk; he wanted to know what I thought. I told him the message was okay, nothing outstanding, but very typical of the preacher's work. I assumed it was the same preacher I had been listening to.

The reply from my friend was interesting. "Did you look to see who actually gave this sermon?" When I looked at the CD I realized that it was not the preacher I had become so used to listening to, but someone he was discipling. Evidently, during this process the disciple had picked up the same intonation, mannerisms, and content as the preacher. While it was obvious he'd become a virtual carbon copy of his mentor, I couldn't help but wonder if he had actually become any more like Jesus.

This kind of discipleship is not found in the Bible, yet it is often what we observe today. We find people making disciples of themselves, not necessarily of Jesus. In light of this, when I search the Scriptures I can't help but come to the conclusion that *we are not called to disciple people.*[2] The desire to do so says much more about the human propensity to make people just like we are, and that is often what we have done.

Everyone should be discipled today in the same way that people were discipled in the first century: by Jesus. The Christian life has changed very little since then. We walk with Jesus, and he trains us in every area of our life, whether we are a construction worker, a secretary, a pastor, or a student. The role of mentors, sages, and guides are similar to the roles of older brothers and sisters who help to guide us in life, but we are not discipled by them. If they are good mentors, sages, and guides, they always point us to Jesus, the real discipler.

In light of this, we must not downplay the role of mentors and community in the discipling process, but they must be put in their proper place. I have been blessed with many older or more experienced people in my life, and I wouldn't trade them for the world. But knowing their depth of knowledge and experience makes it easy for me to start seeking them and not Jesus. We need to be sure that we balance our desire to explore the wisdom of even the most experienced members of our community with the actual goal of discipleship: allowing these people to guide us to Christ.

Paul models the discipleship process for us through his epistles. His call for people to follow him as he follows Christ is a call to discipleship with Christ, not with Paul. Paul is the older brother who wants to help guide us to Christ more effectively. We, on the other hand, are often much more adept at making our own disciples than we are at helping to mold Christ's.

My desire to be discipled by someone meant I wanted to be attached to someone "successful." I might not have realized this at the time, and I probably couldn't have verbalized it, but it was true. Many of us are much more comfortable finding our identity in Christ through other people than directly in Christ himself. Many congregations are based more upon people being in some kind of relationship (however minimal) with the head pastor and, therefore, following him more than they are following Christ. The devastation this can have to a community is obvious once the pastor leaves and the church falls apart.

In a historical study of ancient Judaism, Michael Wilkins says, "For Jews in the Old Testament all discipleship relations were supposed to lead to discipleship to God alone. Now that God had come to earth in Jesus, the true disciple was to focus on him alone. The true disciple was to know Jesus so well, to follow him so closely, that the ultimate goal was to be conformed to his image (cf. Rom. 8:28–29)."[3] This is our calling: to focus on God and not men.

The church's call, on the other hand, is to help people navigate their lives with Christ. This is the discipleship the church is in the business of doing—helping each other turn to God—which is exactly what we see Mark helping us do in his Gospel. But helping each other navigate our spiritual lives and helping each other turn to God are relational tasks and can't merely be preached upon or spun into a program. We can preach the content of discipleship, but how is it possible to teach something through information that is only completely understood through relationship? The discipleship process needs to be lived in community with the goal of abiding in Christ, and it should be understood as a journey into the abundant life.

> We must continually ask ourselves if we are following someone who is a charismatic leader or if we are following Christ.

To help churches determine if they're pointing disciples in the right direction, Wilkins developed four questions that churches need to ask, and these questions can easily be asked of ourselves as well:

1. Are we making disciples of our *institutions*, or are our institutions making *disciples of Jesus*?
2. Are our disciples proficient at *programs* or at living a radical *relationship* with Jesus?
3. Does our attachment to our institutions *isolate* us from the world or *equip* us for changing the world?
4. Are people focusing on *us* because of the importance of our programs, or are we—and our programs—the "means to the end" so that people see *Jesus* more clearly?[4]

Too often the big names bring the big crowds, and rhetoric and charisma excite and titillate audiences in the name of the gospel. We must continually ask ourselves if we are following someone who is a charismatic leader or if we are following Christ.

In Jesus: The Body of Christ

In talking about discipleship in our churches and personal lives, the topic of community is essential. We may still have relationships that are more programmatic or established specifically as "discipling" relationships, but as we have seen above, all of our relationships with other believers should be a part of the discipling process. This can be anything from an older woman explaining prudence to a younger man, to passionate youth reigniting the zeal of the Christians who are tired. But as individuals, we often have good motives and still orient the discipleship process around our own desires and charisma. In understanding the biblical mandate for community, we should come to see ourselves humbly, as one among many in the processes of the body.

It is because of the great capacity we have for influencing others that we need to take "body living" seriously. All too often the task of growing as a disciple is hindered because of activities, committees, meetings, services, and the like, and often that is where we focus our time, money, and effort rather than on spiritual growth. The church's task is to help us as individuals to function as a body and equip us for the work of ministry. And showing us yet again the value God places on "body living," it is within community that Jesus disciples us. He may work directly on us, on us through others, or through us for others, but regardless, his work is accomplished as the body works together.

There are a number of ways in which we may unintentionally foil Jesus's discipling work on our lives. Sometimes we as individuals are to blame. We may find ourselves coming to meet him filled with assumptions and presuppositions and not fully ready for what he has to say. But our communities can be the culprit too. Critique or admonition may be given without a spirit of humility or love. A lack of community that is truly deep may be the problem, since without it few individuals are willing to broach the subject of starting a redemptive community with others who lack significant community interaction. Or we may be in a community that is slowly growing lax in the way the individuals within it are interacting, and it becomes much easier to let everyone deal with their own spirituality and relationship with Jesus in private. Within Christianity, there is no such thing as a private prayer life, private growth, or a private walk with God. All of these things are always done in the context of community.

> The depth and quality of our growth will depend on the community that surrounds us.

In the same sense we are not discipled in private, but Jesus disciples us *in* the world. The community of people around us is the incubator in which we grow. The depth and quality of our growth will depend on the community that surrounds us. This is why Paul's writings are full of references to being one-minded and unified. Christians are people on a mission of holiness, and holiness is a community endeavor. This is why it is important to understand community in terms of believers around us, around the world, and throughout history. We are all on this mission together. My brother's sin affects how I grow, and my sin affects him. All of life is a body issue.

Unfortunately, community also allows us to take other forms of discipleship and mimic ways that do not fit into the theology of discipleship that Jesus offered. We have opened the door for our own gurus—the people whose books, CDs, websites, and churches draw people into what it "really" means to follow Jesus. People begin to fantasize about how great life would be if they could just be discipled by the newest, greatest guru. Christians spend huge amounts of money to sit at the feet of their favorite experts.

There is nothing wrong with seeking out wise counsel from older, more experienced Christians or people who have devoted themselves to studying the Scriptures, but when we sit at another's feet—that is, when we devote ourselves heart and soul to one person—this says a lot about what we believe. It means that we believe our church body has nothing to offer us and that we just don't buy into Jesus's model of discipleship; we have to find a role model to emulate. Discipleship skewed in this way becomes elitist, taking on a rabbinic flavor, where people brag about which leader they have learned from. The Christian model of discipleship always sets us at the feet of Jesus and no other. We may learn from our fellow sisters and brothers who also sit at Jesus's feet, but we are never followers of them.

Discipleship is done within the body of believers. The body, whose individual parts differ greatly, allows us to abide in Jesus with greater depth and intimacy and helps in the process of our worldview deconstruction. In discipleship, we are learning to walk the Jesus way of life with the people he has put in our lives.

To Jesus: Setting Our Eyes on the Goal

Throughout my time walking with Christ, there have been several distinct stages that I can discern. In my youth, Jesus was God who had become man to die on the cross so that

I could go to heaven when I died. Later, Jesus became an object for me to study, someone that I gave my mind to but who didn't mean anything for my life. After that, I started seeing Jesus as a teacher and myself as his apprentice.

While the exact wording or characteristics may vary from person to person, I think that many of us find ourselves in stages similar to these at some point in our lives. As I look back, I see how futile each phase was. No matter what I was doing to advance my understanding of discipleship, *I* was still the focus of it all, and Jesus was secondary.

Even the idea that we are Jesus's apprentices, which has become popular as of late, puts the focus on us, even if we say we are learning to be like Jesus. The goal of an apprenticeship is to develop certain abilities so that we're able to function apart from our master; apprentices are meant to move on to independence at some point.[5] The focus becomes our skill and ability to function and adapt. The most fundamental reason why creating disciples has proven to be so elusive for the North American church is that all of our ideas, programs, and methods for discipleship put ourselves at the end rather than Jesus. The goal of discipleship should always be Jesus and never spiritual skill. Just as the goal of marriage is deeper intimacy and love between husband and wife and never our marital skill, the goal of discipleship is relational depth with Christ.

If we focus on Jesus only as our teacher, he will fail to be a way of life.[6] Our life is *for* Jesus, *with* Jesus, and *toward* Jesus; it is not *about* what Jesus can do for me, even if it means trying to be like him. Our trying to be like Jesus will most often end with our *trying*, not abiding. Since our only chance to be like Jesus stems from abiding in him to begin with (John 15:5), we must approach discipleship with the recognition that our role is abiding, and Jesus's role is growing.

Our natural human propensity will be toward making everything else in our lives *ends* in and of themselves instead of *means* that focus us on God. We will become legalistic about the means we use to get to God—whether they be a church service, a quiet time structure, or style of prayer—and focus on those rather than God. We have taken some great concepts (e.g., confession) and turned them into ways to deal with our sin (what Dallas Willard calls the "gospel of sin management"). Our desire to deal with sin often stems from our desire to feel better about ourselves, to stop feeling guilty, and to avoid depression. Dealing with sin becomes a secondary issue when we come to Jesus, and all that we do should bring us to him. Jesus is the end *and* the means.

> God will unravel our view of reality if we are open to it.

It will be a struggle to walk with Jesus as the first disciples did; they watched their concept of redemption unravel before their very eyes. God will unravel our view of reality if we are open to it. As disciples we are called to follow regardless of our understanding. Jesus will take us on a journey through what we really believe about him, how we really think, and how much we depend on ourselves over him. Discipleship will entail walking the way of the cross with the one who is resurrected and confessing that we care more about bearing fruit and *looking* Christian than abiding in him, about having an experience rather than a relationship, and about having him on our terms rather than on his.

Our desire to have God on our terms, and our confidence in our own self-sufficiency, will be a constant struggle in our discipling relationship with Christ unless we allow him to deconstruct our hearts. Ana-Maria Rizzuto, in her psychological study of how people formulate their understandings of God, says this: "No child arrives at the 'house of God' without his pet God under his arm."[7] She paints a picture of how we all come to God, with our own "god" that we have created through our upbringing, our culture, our context, and so forth. But there always comes a time when that god comes face-to-face with the real God. It is at this point in our lives—not only at conversion, but throughout the process of discipleship—where the pet-god we have grown to love is deconstructed by the true God.

If we follow Jesus only as his apprentices, we will inevitably cease to abide in him for our growth and will turn to autonomy in order to try to live out the Christian message. In doing so, we will neglect Jesus's claim that "apart from Me you can do nothing" (John 15:5). Our life will easily slip into a life of tweaking external aspects of what we do, how we act, plus all the rest, and we will buy into a self-help model for the Christian life. We will fight to conform our externals, rather than relationally growing in intimacy with Christ and allowing the externals to be metamorphosed from within.

Prior to meeting Jesus, Peter and the rest of the disciples certainly knew about grace—even God's grace—but until then they couldn't live from it. Likewise, Paul knew about the forgiveness of God as a Pharisee, which is why he spent time at the temple. He would have seen the temple and the law as manifestations of God's mercy and grace upon him. But until the moment he met Jesus, Paul couldn't live *from* that reality; he had to try to live *toward* it. Paul walked the road to Damascus with his pet-god under his arm, but it was on that road that his god came face-to-face with the real God. In the words of John Calvin, "It is certain that man never achieves a clear knowledge of himself unless he has first looked upon God's face, and then descends from contemplating him to scrutinizing himself."[8] Paul could now fall into the embrace of Jesus because he had come to know who he was in light of who God is. He *knew* humility, not conceptually, but within himself.

A constant struggle in discipleship is walking the balance between the fact that we are good trees and that we need to become good trees. Paul offered us this tension as well, saying that *we have died with Christ*, and now we are to live *as though we had died with Christ* (Romans 6). We may think that, since we are good trees, the Christian life means doing things we are supposed to do. But here we fail to realize that *becoming* a good tree is not a one-time event in our life, but a lifestyle. In the same way that abiding in Christ never ceases to be the Christian life, becoming a good tree never ceases to be the first step in any issue of discipleship. Discipleship will not end like apprenticeship where we become the master;[9] it will always grow toward deeper and deeper dependence on the only Master, Jesus.

DISCIPLESHIP FROM WITHIN

In my own life, understanding the reality that Christ has already accomplished my deliverance, adoption, and acceptance, all before I was born, has proven to be the key change I've made that has allowed me to finally see fruit. For much of my life I worked extremely hard at the Christian life and failed at it miserably. Until that point, I could not possibly hear or understand the message that Jesus came to give. I still thought I could do it on my own. My failure was essential to finally understanding discipleship, as was coming to understand Paul's main message that the law is not enough because it is external to us. It is only through Jesus and the sending of his Spirit that we can come to live *by* the source of Jesus's own life, the Spirit of God. His message of grace through faith was one of union through sacrifice—Jesus's sacrifice, and yet we often continue to try to make it work on our own.

> We can find freedom in Christ only from understanding that he is calling us to a relationship with himself, rather than is looking for slave labor.

This is when I began to see my pet-god come forth. I didn't want what Jesus offered. I wanted glory. Jesus's call to walk the way of the cross meant nothing to me. My understanding of the Christian life revolved around seeing evangelical rock stars, those whose lives were lived in the limelight. I wanted that, but I never wanted what Jesus offered. It was only when I heard my own personal version of "This is a difficult message, who can listen to it?" (see John 6:60) come out of my mouth that I was truly able to open up to Jesus and respond as Peter did: "Lord, to whom shall we go? You have words of eternal life" (v. 68). Naturally, I wanted an exciting life; I wanted to masculinize the gospel by making it an adrenaline rush, and I wanted to have my path grow increasingly easy and fruitful. Instead, Jesus brought me to himself.

We can find freedom in Christ only from understanding that he is calling us to a relationship with himself, rather than looking for slave labor. It can be easy to focus all of our attention on the bearing of fruit and forget that fruit comes from an abiding relationship with Jesus. Of course, Jesus knew and predicted that people would do this; it is in our nature. Therefore, right after teaching about good trees producing good fruit, Jesus offers this aside:

Not everyone who says to Me, "Lord, Lord," will enter the kingdom of heaven, but he who does the will of My Father who is in heaven will enter. Many will say to Me on that day, "Lord, Lord, did we not prophesy in Your name, and in Your name cast out demons, and in Your name perform many miracles?" And then I will declare to them, "I never knew you; depart from Me, you who practice lawlessness."

Matthew 7:21–23

After focusing on bearing fruit, it would be an easy mistake to turn the Christian life into following rules and acting a certain way, trying to make that the path to bearing fruit. But what then would our response be to Jesus? Merely an impersonal résumé of things done in the name of the Lord. Even though the list may be impressive and the acts accomplished miraculous, Jesus *will not know us*. The failure of our lives would not be what we did or did not accomplish but the fact that we thought the acts would get us somewhere.

In the next paragraph (Matt. 7:24–27), Jesus goes on to teach about the man who hears his words and acts on them being like a wise man who builds his house on a rock. The rock is Jesus, and the man who is a disciple of Jesus abides in him and knows him. In return, the disciple is known by Jesus. The man who has to read off his résumé to Jesus is giving an exposition of his foundation, and in the face of Jesus, that foundation quickly shows itself to be sand.

This area could be the one in which evangelicals have made the greatest mistake. With all of the change that has taken place (and continues to take place) within evangelicalism, we have had ample opportunity to shift our focus from how we function to how we abide. But sadly, we have continued to focus on our programs and policies instead of pointing each other to Jesus. The community of disciples—the church—needs to be the place where life is different.

During the times I have traveled around the country to speak, I have been amazed at how the stories everyone related to were the saddest stories I told. Everyone was able to commiserate when I talked about the dryness that the Christian life can bring, and everyone nodded in agreement when I talked about being burned out. This surprised me at the time. How could it be that the people with the most resources, the greatest opportunity to find God, and the most freedom in their religion were so empty?

FOR JESUS: LIVING FROM THE END

I started to wonder why the Christian life seemed like such a massive burden when Jesus talked about his yoke being easy and his burden light. Every time I tried something new I felt like I was hitting a wall. I was trying to move forward, but I had no idea what direction "forward" was. And I knew I wasn't alone.

When I was young, my family often chose kid-friendly restaurants when we went out to eat. These restaurants usually provided a placemat and crayons for little ones. The placemats were filled with things to color, games to play, and so on. My favorite thing to do was the maze. The thing is, I was never very good at those mazes. They always seemed like they should be relatively easy: just go until you hit a wall. But I tended to look at the maze as a whole, filled with dead ends, tricks, and false paths. I knew that every maze had a path that would take you to the very end, but as I surveyed the various paths I could take, hitting a wall seemed inevitable.

This is an adequate metaphor for the way many people live the Christian life. We have all taken various paths promising freedom, victory, and even blessings, but we now know these were false starts. We have tried hard at the Christian life, but it just hasn't worked out the way we expected.

Back to the maze. I quickly learned that starting from the end made it infinitely easier. Particularly with the simplistic mazes on the back of those placemats, starting at the end led directly to the beginning. The Christian life is very similar. In fact, Jesus specifically revealed the end to us in order to fix our eyes ahead to where the path was leading so we would not lose our way.

Jesus revealed the end in several places, but I would like to focus on one specifically. Going back to the Gospel of Mark, we find Jesus once again doing something peculiar.

> On reaching Jerusalem, Jesus entered the temple area and began driving out those who were buying and selling there. He overturned the tables of the money changers and the benches of those selling doves, and would not allow anyone to carry merchandise through the temple courts. And as he taught them, he said, "Is it not written: 'My house will be called a house of prayer for all nations'? But you have made it 'a den of robbers.'"
>
> Mark 11:15–17 NIV

So how does this reveal the end? Jesus was taking on the role of a prophet.[10] He was enacting the temple destruction in his actions against the money changers, and he was giving the reasons in his speech. The people of God are to be a blessing to the world; the people of God are to be holy. The people of God were failing.

When we look at the story in context, we see that Mark uses two stories about a fig tree to bracket the temple story. On his way to Jerusalem, Jesus became hungry and looked for some figs on a fig tree that was in full bloom. When he found it was fruitless, he cursed the tree (Mark 11:12–14).

Later, after the temple incident, Peter notices that the fig tree is withered from the roots up (Mark 11:20–21). This fig tree gives us Mark's interpretation of the temple. Jesus went to the temple when it was in full function—people bustling everywhere, priests doing their thing, the temple tax being collected; you could say that it was in full leaf. The temple looked in every way as if it were bearing fruit—but, to Jesus's way of thinking, it was fruitless. And just as Jesus cursed and withered the tree for not bearing fruit, Jesus curses the temple and declares it "withering," or in other words, on its way to destruction—a description that would be fulfilled less than forty years later.

Jesus's critique of the temple, and the Jewish leadership behind the temple, was that it was fruitless. The root system was bad—the temple failed to abide in its source of life and nourishment. It failed to be what it was supposed to be and in fact had become a place for the unrepentant and immoral to hide (a robber's den). The temple was seen as a place where you do religious things to make up for the fact that your life was not lived for God. As disciples, we are to live knowing this can just as easily be a reality for us today and that the same question Jesus posed to the temple, "Are you bearing fruit?" will be posed to us. As Jesus states in John 15:

> I am the true vine, and My Father is the vinedresser. Every branch in Me that does not bear fruit, He takes away; and every branch that bears fruit, He prunes it so that it may bear more fruit. . . . Abide in Me, and I in you. As the branch cannot bear fruit of itself unless it abides in the vine, so neither can you unless you abide in Me. I am the vine, you are the branches; he who abides in Me and I in him, he bears much fruit, for apart from Me you can do nothing. If anyone does not abide in Me, he is thrown away as a branch and dries

up; and they gather them, and cast them into the fire and they are burned.

John 15:1–2, 4–6

The burden of the disciple is that of abiding. Too many have continually left prayer and God behind to take on the world by themselves, and too often they end up creating kingdoms without God, trees without fruit, and temples that fail to abide.

The other lesson to take from the temple story is that the path we walk with Jesus is not directionless, but results in mission. As the new temple, the community of believers stands as the light to the world, the place where the foreigners, widows, and orphans find a home. It is within the community of believers living out the kingdom as the living temple that we see the world change. As Jesus's disciples clamored over themselves trying to change the world, they had to realize that their actions were only kingdom actions when they were born as fruit from abiding. They had to continue to walk with Jesus, even when they could no longer see him, no longer watch him, and no longer hear audibly his rebuke.

As fellow disciples, we must realize this as well. In passages like the one above Jesus points us to the end of time when we will stand before him as fruit-bearing branches. We should not be afraid, for Jesus tells us to rest in his grace and assures us that "there is therefore now no condemnation for those who are in Christ Jesus" (Rom. 8:1). We will stand at the judgment, hearing the words "no condemnation," and instead of feeling the need to spout off our résumé, we will know that there is nothing for us to say. All has been said in the work of Christ. All discipleship starts from this place of redemption and is able to move forward in freedom toward intimacy with the one who loved us first. It is out of this intimacy that we have a vision for the world cast before our eyes: that the people of God would be the blessing of the world, that all might come to know who the Lord is.

11

MISSION

Community of Light

There are few things closer to the heart of God than people on a mission to do his will. As we have already seen, God promised Abraham that his descendants would bless the world, and through faith we are Abraham's children. Therefore, as we journey with Christ we have to understand that abiding in him will produce good fruit and that, through our abiding, we will be salt and light in the world. Yet often the fruit we bear is not the kind we were expecting—I doubt Peter understood that his good fruit would lead to martyrdom, at least not when he first started out. But as we submit our understanding of the kingdom to God, he will show us the kingdom way, and it is through this way that the world will be changed.

In being missional we turn our eyes to kingdom values instead of focusing on what we get out of Christianity for ourselves. It is at the very core of worldview formation. Unfortunately, we seem to get stuck somewhere along the journey, and we judge the kingdom based on secular values rather than kingdom values. Our mission often looks remarkably similar to the mission of McDonald's, Starbucks, and even our country's foreign policy.

> If we can't live kingdom values among ourselves, we have no chance of being the kingdom to the world.

The dilemma we cannot ignore is that for even our largest churches, the area surrounding them rarely feels the effect of the thousands of disciples who gather there.[1] There is no evidence that areas with megachurches—or even just a large number of churches—are less materialistic, less selfish, or even less immoral. Notice that I did not start with what might be typical missional points about the homeless, the poor, or other needs. Those issues are extremely important and should be central to what the church is doing, but the mission of the church is a communal one, and the first sign that we are a sick tree will be that we have failed to live out kingdom values among ourselves, let alone in the world.

If we can't live kingdom values among ourselves, we have no chance of being the kingdom to the world. As we will see, turning inward is the first step toward being missional. It is by turning inward that we might actually be a blessing to the world. The desire to "fix" the world's problems and solve society's problems is often the same psychological drive that causes men to build massive companies, be in control, and be seen as valuable. Our first and natural inclination is external rather than internal, but the way of Jesus necessitates a movement inwards to be effective outwardly. Any mission that does not start with the community of believers fails to take seriously that kingdom values grow out of a developmental journey of a people. If our communities are in shambles, our mission is as well. That is why the first step in being missional is being communal.

A New Mission: Community Faithfulness

For a while, ministry in North America was not really seen as missional activity. The society seemed too Christian to be considered a viable place for mission work. But often it's the places we expect to be strongholds for the faith that are the places that are destroyed by decay from the inside out. A friend used the poignant metaphor of an oak tree that is rotted inside—it looks massive and powerful from the outside, but it lacks life and growth.

As my friends went on to do missions on secular college campuses around the country, I decided to try my hand at a Christian school. Few places seem to need a missionary less than a Christian school, but as anyone who has attended one will tell you, they are the easiest places to grow inner rot. Knowing that I didn't just want to affect the school but the areas outside the school—the city, the churches, the poor—I started meeting with a small group of guys. I started small, rather than broadcasting the group to the entire school, because I believe kingdom power stems from small groups of community whose aim is devotion to God and each other. In order to do this well, we adopted a principle:[2] don't tell people about what we are doing. Our driving purpose was not to change the world but to find God. Our assumption was that the more we became a community that was honestly searching for God, the more the world would be changed.

Our concern was not to be evangelistic but to be the kingdom. What made this experiment personally interesting was that, if it worked, it would have worked in the worst possible scenario. What kind of impact can you have when those around you already believe?

Much of this was experimental. We were not necessarily concerned with following biblical patterns of what a "church" is; we had our own churches already and weren't interested in starting another one. We were trying to be the clan of God, the people of God in a given location. Church wasn't the issue; the issue was the kingdom. Our concerns did not have to do with what people wanted; we weren't trying to satisfy their desires, nor were we concerned with the questions people were asking. We were concerned with answers to the questions people *were not yet asking but should be*. We were attempting to contextualize the gospel in our very persons—we wanted to incarnate the message of Christ within our community, through the realization of the kingdom among ourselves.

Our idea of mission was based on our group being conquered by God (an issue to be taken up below) and bearing the evidence of his Spirit working. At first this required little from us other than devotion to God and the understanding that we would be his voice and love in the world. We were testing Lesslie Newbigin's assumption that "the great missionary proclamations in Acts are not given on the unilateral initiative of the apostles but in response to questions asked by others, *questions prompted by the presence of something which calls for explanation*."[3] If we have nothing terribly impressive or powerful to be asked about, then what were we doing anyway? Our assumption was that, if we lived out the kingdom life through the Spirit's power and not our own, it would be so obvious that not talking about it would be irrelevant—people would demand to know what we were up to.

We realized that the mission of God had to overtake us before we could bring others into it. This brought up several issues, specifically because we were trying to model what happened in Acts. A major concern was that we were not being true to the early church's ideal by addressing ourselves first and others later. But, as we have discussed, this is precisely what was modeled in Acts, not to the neglect of those outside, but to their advantage. We knew all the canned answers to their questions; we could spout off our testimonies, but unless we had a community to bring them into, and unless we were living out the kingdom reality, these abilities would be fruitless. As put by Newbigin:

> In discussions about the contemporary mission of the Church it is often said that the Church ought to address itself to the real questions which people are asking. That is to misunderstand the mission of Jesus and the mission of the Church. The world's questions are not the questions which lead to life. What really needs to be said is that where the Church is faithful to its Lord, there the powers of the kingdom are present and people begin to ask the question to which the gospel is the answer. And that, I suppose, is why the letters of St. Paul contain so many exhortations to faithfulness but no exhortations to be active in mission.[4]

What Newbigin hits on so strongly here is that community faithfulness was Paul's (a missionary and missional person if there ever was one) main desire for the people of God. Paul's assumption was that if faithful communities are established, then they will be the light on the hill and out of those communities will come people of mission: people who have God's burden for the world on their hearts and who will impact it because of that. Theirs will be a powerful mission because they will be able to call others *into* a community of faithfulness. The idea of being "in Christ" will mean more to people who see the gospel incarnated within a community of believers.

I do not see this happening in the church today. When I became a Christian I felt as though I no longer mattered. Even though I didn't have a community, an understanding of what Christianity was really about, any knowledge about the workings of the Spirit, and so forth, I was told that my job was now to go out and get others. I hadn't been called into the people of God; I had been called into a multilevel marketing scheme. Fruit, for many churches, is labor. If people are doing things for the church, evangelizing, or giving money, then it is assumed they are incarnating the gospel. Unfortunately, we have thousands of people who did not sign up for community, incarnating the gospel, or being a light to the world. We have people who signed up because they thought it would allow them to be what they have always wanted to be: successful, put together, and happy.

Newbigin's point is that the mission to the world starts with the faithfulness of the community. This is why issues of loving one another, unity, one-mindedness, and discipline within the community are central aspects of the New Testament. It is not because we want to have a community that turns in on itself and shuts the world out; it is because the

> Fruit, for many churches, is labor.

community in being faithful will be a light in the darkness. In trying to change the world through power, numbers, money, and programs, we have bought into a false understanding of reality and have failed to take seriously the way Jesus enacted the kingdom.

When I meet with pastors, I am often amazed at (and saddened by) how many people first consider money, numbers, buildings, and bands when contemplating what it means to be "successful." We have to align our understanding of being missional communities with the reality that God's plan to change the world involved three years, twelve guys who usually didn't get it—one of whom walked away—and the brutal death of the guy in charge.

In the book of Acts we see a community that was characterized by teaching (the Word), fellowship (community), breaking of bread (remembering the way of the cross), and a life of prayer (Spirit). We are told that this community acted as if they really were a family: sharing all things, selling things to give money to one another, and sharing meals and the Lord's Supper together. Like an ancient family, they were of one mind and continued to live out their "typical" lives, which meant that as Jews they still went to the temple. Their unity and love for one another was public knowledge, even though the activities that led to it (teaching, fellowship, sharing all things, etc.) might not have been as public.

There was certainly something different about this people. We are told by Luke that "the Lord added to their number daily" (Acts 2:47 NIV). This is a communal statement. They were embodying the kingdom, and people were entering it because of that. It is just as we are told in John that men will know we are disciples if we love one another (John 13:35). Acts 2 shows us what this really looks like.

With the increase in size, it would have been very easy for the community to grow too large to continue the family approach. But when the family started bearing the bad fruit of becoming a movement rather than a family, the apostles put seven men in charge to make sure that people did not fall through the cracks (Acts 6:1–7). While the apostles themselves focused on the ministry of the Word, they refused to forget that community health was a major issue in the growth, development, and mission of the people of God. Likewise, if we step back and look at Paul's ministry, just as Newbigin tells us, Paul focuses on faithfulness, community health, discipline, love, and unity—the aspects of community and family life—more than almost anything else.

There are three misunderstandings about community that may arise in light of this. The first is equating focus on the community with being self-centered. A focus on community health is imperative in pointing community members to God, and it is in our relationship with God that we come to engage his mission in the world—in *his* way, not our own. That is the path of growth to which God has called us. If any community fails to make the missional turn, we must remember that the solution is not to get them to do something, but to get them back to God. Failing to be missional points to the inner health of the tree, and so the solution must treat the roots, not the branches.

Second, we may think that being in this kind of community means we must always have the desire to support everyone else and "be there" for everyone. But just as with any other kind of relationship, there will be many times when we will not want to care for others, when giving seems like a burden, and when outsiders are a pain. And that's okay. God knows us better than we know ourselves, so it doesn't help to pretend this isn't the case.[5] We need to bring these things to God because he is the only one who can change our heart. What this does *not* mean is that we can wait until the desire to do these things appears. We should give even when we don't feel like it but, as we do so, recognize what is really going on in our hearts. The kingdom solution isn't to mimic kingdom values but to continue on the path of becoming the type of people who *do* desire to do these things because of who we are at our core: disciples of Jesus.

A third misunderstanding can be illustrated by something that happened to me the other day. I recently ran into an old friend who had become a Christian. I was excited about how much he had grown spiritually, although there was still a strong sense of his old pride, arrogance, and judgmental behavior. It didn't bother me that he still had old habits; he was bound to. What was important was that he was growing and deepening in his faith and understanding of himself. Yet his behavior pointed to a deeper reality that immature and mature Christians alike struggle with. He judged other Christians, even questioning if they were saved, based on how much they looked like him. That was his plumb line. He defined Christianity by who he was and who he wanted to become, and anyone who didn't fit that mold was considered questionable. So the third possible misunderstanding is to think that we who are in these communities and engaging in spiritual formation are justified in thinking other Christians are doomed to fruitless, growthless lives because clearly our framework, behavior, and method are *the* ways to be Christian.

The minute we start judging ourselves and each other based on secular or personal standards, we have failed to have kingdom sight. Yet we do this kind of thing every day in our churches, in our prayers, and in our relationships. The more guilt and shame motivate us, the harder it will be to have a

> The minute we start judging ourselves and each other based on secular or personal standards, we have failed to have kingdom sight.

powerful mission to the world, because it will be harder to have a real and honest relationship with God. We must remember that "the fruit of the Spirit is love, joy, peace, patience, kindness, goodness, faithfulness, gentleness, self-control," (Gal. 5:22–23), and we only bear these fruits through the love of Christ.

In the book of Acts, as well as the later correspondence between believers, there is evidence of these three misunderstandings. We can't assume that we won't struggle with them as well. In looking back on the earliest communities, it seems that their unity around a common mission of faithfulness to God within the world was a greater and more fundamental issue to them than their individual disagreements. Their focus on community faithfulness was a bright light in a dark world, and that was the launching point for their mission; they could now call for justice, peace, and unity because they had lived these kingdom values in a world that was desperate for them.

The Casting of a New Mission: Counting the Cost

When my minicommunity group started, we tried to find our vision for community life in Acts. We were looking for the ideology of the earliest believers, not seeking to copy their behaviors. We realized that we lived in a very different time, with different social, economic, and even relational issues. Our concern wasn't becoming like them in action but like them in spirit.

Since the group we started was not a church, and because we had a very specific mission in mind, we made getting in very hard. It wasn't that we restricted membership, but we did try to talk people out of wanting to join. We required a good amount of time for meeting, relating, and communing, and everyone had a brother whose sole goal was to know the depths of his brother's heart and love him in it. If someone wasn't up for this kind of community, there were no hard feelings and we didn't look down on them. Anyone who wanted to enter would first have to count the cost of entering—wouldn't it be worse to continually have to separate the group from a member because he didn't realize what he was in for? Yet this is what happens in the church all the time.

We didn't expect perfection from each other, nor did we expect anyone to fully live up to the standards we had set—that wasn't the point. We just wanted to be up front about what our expectations were. We knew it would be hard, and it was going to take a lot of life change to live this way. We knew that people were not used to relating with anyone on the level we were asking. But on the other hand, we let them know that if they weren't on board with our mission, that was fine; we would still be their friends, and we wouldn't think less of them. We knew that what we were doing was totally outside the realm of what most people considered the Christian life to be, and until they saw it, they wouldn't understand why we demanded such a commitment.

In this sense, we actually modeled our philosophy of membership on Jesus's way of evangelizing. In Luke 14:25 Jesus turns to the "crowds" (which signifies that he was speaking to those who are curious but not yet committed—the first "seekers" if you will) and gives them his message of evangelism by saying, "If anyone comes to Me, and does not hate his own father and mother and wife and children and brothers and sisters, yes, and even his own life, he cannot be my disciple. Whoever does not carry his own cross and come after Me cannot be My disciple. For which one of you, when he wants to build a tower, does not first sit down and calculate the cost to see if he has enough to complete it?" (Luke 14:26–28).[6] Jesus wants people to think through the decisions they make, knowing that the community will only be effective if they are *all* interested in the journey he wants to bring them on.

Jesus's statement is raw and without explanation. Just as in John 6:52–65, Jesus doesn't feel the need to explain himself; he simply offers the reality of his message and waits for a response. Committing to Jesus would necessitate a break from family, traditions, beliefs, and assumptions, so Jesus is making sure people have counted the cost for this journey. Likewise, we wanted to be straightforward with the reality to which we were calling people. They were not their own, they were bought with a price, and their actions, even (and especially) in "private" areas, were community issues.

Jesus allowed those who were only curious to journey along, and welcomed them to do so, but he did not allow them to have an unrealistic view of the Christian commitment. I think he recognized the importance of living out his message and relationship with the disciples in front of and with the crowd, which was probably the most powerful message in and of itself. On the other hand, he knew that people would want to join them without counting the cost, and when they began the journey of deconstruction, those people would be overwhelmed and would cease to continue on. It is no wonder, then, that he ends his speech with the question, "If even salt has become tasteless, with what will it be seasoned?" (Luke 14:34).

Unfortunately the church has ceased talking about Jesus's message of counting the cost and instead focuses on how much we have to offer (friendship, money, self-esteem, the feeling that we are a part of something big, etc.). It can be easy to sell the church as a means to fill emotional and psychological desires and never actually ask anyone to buy into the work that Christ wants to do in our hearts. In the North American church particularly, we are a people who love to be a part of something exciting but who rarely want to let that change our lifestyle, our views, or our relationships.

After just one semester, we lost three of the twelve guys we started with. It was a very frustrating time because they were willing to walk away not because they differed ideologically, but because they refused to engage in the life of the community. They wanted life on their own terms and wouldn't agree with what our standards of living were. We understood and agreed to try to maintain relationships with them, but at the same time we let them know that we would have to maintain a distinction between what they were about and what we were about.

Because we were not a church, we didn't see our actions toward these three guys as discipline per se. Our desire was to be a place where the kingdom came on earth as it did in heaven, and we knew that if people were there for other reasons, it would never happen. In our quest to be like-minded, we found it necessary to actually work at and take steps, however radical, toward remaining like-minded.

Something interesting happened after that. After seeing our brothers walk away, we became pretty deflated. It felt as if we were wrong, that kingdom living just wasn't something that Christians were interested in anymore. It was at that point that people started asking and even demanding to know what was going on. We started hearing things like, "I don't know what you guys are doing or who you are doing it with, but whatever it is, I want in." Even after telling people what we required and trying to explain that they might not actually want in, we tripled in size. It was not that we were looking to grow or somehow saw growth as the sign of "success." We were working on the assumption that it would take a lot longer for people to catch the kingdom vision in which we were trusting—but God seemed to have something else in mind.

We couldn't help but look back to Acts and see how modeling the ideology in our context was bearing similar fruit. We were meeting each other's needs, acting as family, sharing all, and pointing each other to the Lord—and the Lord added to our numbers. Even after separating from some of our members, we were found attractive by outsiders because of our unity, because we had something that cost us something, and because of what God was doing in our lives. People wanted more than they typically found in half-committed groups where they could slip in and out unnoticed. They wanted a deeper commitment because it helped them to realize what kind of journey they were on. At the time I was taken off guard by the reality that people wanted God to act in their lives as he had in ours. It was our commitment to unity around the values of the kingdom that people wanted, not anything we had to offer them.

We learned a lesson that I have seen reflected in the lives of the people who have changed the face of Christianity. The people we think of when we think of the great evangelists, or individuals who rallied a group to God and not themselves, were not great because of good communication skills or cunning programs but because they were totally reformed by God. I have heard a story about D. L. Moody that illustrates this. As the story goes, someone went to his church to see if he could figure out why Moody's ministry was so effective. When this person left he said that it has to be God, because Moody had no gifts or talents in and of himself. It is the work that God has done in our lives that is effective, not the work we do to become great churches, successful evangelists, or brilliant preachers.

Of all the people in whom this is evident, the apostle Paul seems the perfect example. In all of Paul's writings, the place where this comes through most clearly is in 2 Corinthians. In this letter, Paul states something that is often misunderstood. He says, "But thanks be to God, who always leads us in triumph in Christ, and manifests through us the sweet aroma of the knowledge of Him in every place" (2 Cor. 2:14). At first glance, this verse seems to say that we are the ones in triumph. But this is not possible. Dr. Moyer Hubbard offers a translation that takes into account the background and original language. He renders it this way: "Thanks be to God who always leads us *as conquered foes* in his triumphal procession."[7] This is clearly a very different feel than the first translation!

In the ancient Roman world, after an enemy was conquered, the commanding leader or general of the enemy's armies and the captured troops would be led in chains through Rome in a massive parade, and the conquering general or leader would be celebrated.[8] So when Paul speaks of being led in a triumphal procession, he means we're being led through the world as people conquered by Christ.

But what is the aroma Paul refers to? Dr. Hubbard goes on to explain: "One of the standard features of religious or civic rituals in antiquity was the use of incense and other fragrant materials. . . . In describing the triumphal procession . . . Plutarch tells us that 'every temple was open and filled with garlands and incense.'"[9] Paul is painting a picture that is not only filled with visual imagery, but is also filled with familiar scents. An ancient reader would get a mental picture of being led through Rome as someone conquered, having the aroma from the temples fill the air. Paul goes on to say, "We are a fragrance of Christ to God among those who are being saved and among those who are perishing; to the one an aroma from death to death, to the other an aroma from life to life" (2 Cor. 2:15–16). Paradoxically, the scent for us, the conquered, is life, but those who are convinced our life is a waste will smell death.

> The problem of the church is not that we have failed to be missional but that we have failed to be developmental.

Paul's life was a message that either turned people toward Christ or turned people away from Christ. As we have seen, this is exactly what parables do. In fact, the Christian life is an enacted parable of the kingdom. Just as Jesus's actions in the temple were an enacted parable about God's view of the temple, the Christian life is to be an enacted parable of the kingdom reality.

The problem of the church is not that we have failed to be missional but that we have failed to be developmental. In the words of Newbigin:

> The Church is not so much the agent of the mission as the locus of the mission. It is God who acts in the power of his Spirit, doing mighty works, creating signs of a new age, working secretly in the hearts of men and women to draw them to Christ. When they are so drawn, they become part of a community which claims no masterful control of history, but continues to bear witness to the real meaning and goal of history by a life which—in Paul's words—by always bearing about in the body the dying of Jesus becomes the place where the risen life of Jesus is made available for others (2 Cor. 4:10).[10]

It is through bearing this witness that we can model the power of the kingdom. It was being conquered by God that allowed Paul to be such a powerful minister, apostle, and saint, and it is this conquering that ties together discipleship, mission, and the journey of belief formation.

CONTRASTING MISSIONS: A WAY UNTRIED

In Jesus's cleansing of the temple, one of his major critiques is that they have failed to be a blessing to the world. The people had made *religion* into something to do and activities to partake in, and they had failed to stay connected to the true vine. Somewhere along the line they had forgotten what Hosea prophesied, that the Lord delights "in loyalty rather than sacrifice, and in the knowledge of God rather than burnt offerings" (Hos. 6:6). In our day, the same can be said for many of us.

The evangelical church has been seduced into believing that if we just devote enough time, money, energy, power, and other resources to tasks, preaching, and outreach, we will become a light to the world. Our books and programs have shown that we are much more interested in simple and pragmatic answers to the kingdom than the kingdom itself. Even in our desire to make a difference in the world, we have bought into a methodology that negates the kingdom, and instead mimics the strategies of secular leadership, business, and growth models. In doing so, even in our outreach we show how little we care about a world full of darkness. Light is the only answer for a world in darkness, and the only way to be light is to take the deconstructing work of the Spirit seriously.

In the group that I helped lead, we found that, even though we were surrounded by Christians, the change and development in the group created too much light to go unnoticed. Oddly, it was during the time when we felt most defeated that the work of the Spirit was most obvious. It was the first time I really understood how growth can occur and that it is not the result of my own work but, instead, of my submission. Up until this point, we had tried to grow ourselves. But after that experience, we learned to rest on the communal presence of the Spirit.

It is by the work of the Spirit in the hearts of his people that we will come to bring justice, peace, hope, and love to a world that finds itself increasingly lonely, poor, sick, and hopeless. It is not within the scope of this book to talk about the pragmatic issues or even the methodological issues connected to being missional, but it is clear that we always need more and more people creatively living out these realities. This creativity, however, needs to be curbed by the reality that the mission we are a part of is God's, and our partaking of it will have more to do with what he is doing, has done, and is continuing to do in us than with what we do in the world.

None of this should take away from the need to use words and be ready to give an account. As Newbigin points out, this should, more often than not, come out of the questions people will inevitably ask a kingdom person. Of course there will still be times when that is not the case. There will be times when acting out the kingdom without speaking will be the most appropriate method of bringing God's love, and there will be times when outright proclamation will be. But throughout the New Testament, the movement of the earliest believers was to plant holistic communities who counted the cost of a developmental journey with God. They often struggled and occasionally failed, but they were always encouraged—not for their own sakes, but for God's and the world's.

For the group I was a part of, the turn toward mission came rather quickly, but in different ways than we expected. We still took part in what we expected our mission to look like—meeting with the homeless, the city council, and just loving those the church had left behind. But we also found that because of our initiative, as subdued as we had made it, other groups began to spring up that were looking for guidance. We found that the Christian community was longing for a group to say, like Paul, "Follow me as I follow Christ"—one that was actually embodying the kingdom message as the overriding imperative in life.

> Everywhere around us we have communities that can potentially incarnate the gospel, and it is in those communities that we must start our mission.

Everywhere around us we have communities that can potentially incarnate the gospel, and it is in those communities that we must start our mission. We don't typically find ourselves on Mars Hill like Paul, among pagan philosophers debating worldview, but we may find ourselves in churches like that in Corinth—a family struggling to be devoted to God amid a world that lives by the opposite values. As Paul understood, and as I have come to see, the light that will shine most brightly in that world is shone forth by people on a journey of belief formation—having their whole beings conformed to the likeness of Jesus.

It will always be easier to make mission the center of the Christian life—it makes us feel important. But the purpose of the Christian life, if it is to remain *Christian*, is to grow deeper with Christ, and the result will be a transformed person who is on mission. Yet the purpose is never mission itself. While that may seem like mere semantics, it is a crucial distinction. It is the difference between man's way and God's way. If we are concerned with the kingdom, then we have to engage the kingdom in kingdom ways and not simply do kingdomlike things.

This book was designed to emulate this process. I have ended on mission because it is the fruit of a healthy tree. Hopefully, throughout this process you can see how Jesus formed this ideology and how it was lived out by the earliest believers. Our task is not to just take the ways in which they played this out in their lives and mimic them, but to contextualize them for our situations, knowing that there will be many pitfalls.

One of the greatest pitfalls is doing the things of God for ourselves and failing to do them for God. We are, and continue to be, a people obsessed with success, individuality, power, and pragmatism. In the Bible, we find these values deconstructed and redeveloped into totally new categories. We find a people who see martyrdom as success and power, and who, by turning inward, have actually taken the first step toward being outwardly focused.

I was in a church not too long ago where I saw a large fountain off to the side of the lobby. What caught my attention was that it was a ziggurat, which is an ancient pagan temple and, more importantly, what the Tower of Babel (Genesis 11) would have been. I figured that the children's ministry must have been doing something on Genesis, so I went to look. What I found amazed me. At the base of this huge fountain were boulders, and on the boulders were things the church had accomplished. I couldn't believe a church would actually have a replica of the tower whose construction God forestalled because of human arrogance and that they would put their own accomplishments at its foundation! How does something like this go unnoticed? Too often this kind of pride and arrogance is what defines us; we have become impressed with what we can accomplish on our own.

Usually we are not this obvious in how human-centered we are, but it is lurking beneath the surface regardless. On our own, we can build big buildings, grow large churches and denominations, and even help people around the world. But we can easily do this for ourselves because we want to be successful, important, and a part of something bigger than ourselves. We can end up like the temple Jesus stormed—a sign of success, wealth, and power: bustling with people, but devoid of fruit. What God offers us is much more but in a much different way. We enter the kingdom by kingdom means, for kingdom ends, and for kingdom purposes and never by our own accomplishments.

> Until we truly come to believe that God's way is actually the best way even when it seems backwards and inconsistent, we will continue to build empires rather than kingdoms, make converts rather than disciples, and become successful rather than holy.

When we look at how we have typically approached the Christian life and the life of the church, it is easy to see how we have done so according to man's way and not God's way. It is no surprise that we have failed to make a significant difference in our culture when this has been our plan. When we commit to a journey of belief formation with Christ, we are doing so with an understanding that we will be transformed, reformed, and renewed to a vision of life that lives according to kingdom values. Until we truly come to believe that God's way is actually the best way even when it seems backwards and inconsistent, we will continue to build empires rather than kingdoms, make converts rather than disciples, and become successful rather than holy.

In this sense, the evangelical church should be overburdened by our lack of unity. If unity is one of the central facets of being a holy people, then our being missional must start there. When as a church we value our own independence, focus on our own problems, and mimic what others in our area are doing, we tend to ignore the people of God in our given location. If we are honestly a people of mission, we must also be a people devoted to finding unity in our common quest for Jesus.

G. K. Chesterton once said, "The Christian ideal has not been tried and found wanting; it has been found difficult and left untried."[11] This is where we remain today. The Christian way seems too counterintuitive, too risky, and too heavy a burden to bear. But we believe this not because we have tried it but because we assume we won't be able to handle it. Yet acknowledging this limitation is the first step in the right direction—we cannot do it on our own, nor should we even try. We are on a journey toward being able to say from the core of who we are, "Without Christ, we can do nothing."

EPILOGUE

A Vision for the Future

When I am left on my own and my journey is decided on my terms and with my direction, I always end up with a different god than the Bible's, a serene and simpler Jesus, and a view of Christianity that looks more like me than it does like God. Even worse, I often fail to notice.

Throughout this book I have offered the metaphor of a journey to describe the Christian life. But the idea of *journey* will not encapsulate this fully. We can be journeying with anyone, going anywhere, and be far removed from the Christian life. As I have stated in several places, and what many have said before me, is that the Christian journey looks most like a marriage.

As we journey with and toward God, we are brought into his family through his love, and we grow as we are in his love as well. Like a marriage, though, it quickly becomes clear how much baggage we bring to the table. While our partner may accept us anyway, we should enter into a journey of formation that will allow us to love more fully and more selflessly.

> The danger in talking about a relationship with Christ and the spiritual life in a book is that the medium is not very relational.

In a marriage, it can often be easier to buy gifts, to avoid arguments, or to provide financially than to look at what is really going on in each other's heart. Once deeper issues are opened, we have to be ready to deal with our fears, sins, guilt, shame, and selfishness. The easy solution is to avoid that and just move on. While this feels better, and indeed feels like forward motion, it actually sends us backwards. Likewise, on the Christian journey the easy solution is to avoid changing our views, to avoid looking at who we truly are, and to just accomplish things as a way to deflect the work God has to do in our hearts. It is much easier to start "doing things for God" and try to prove our value than to stand naked in front of him. But part of faith is knowing that in him, regardless of whether we feel like it, we are immensely valuable.

The danger in talking about a relationship with Christ and the spiritual life in a book is that the medium is not very relational. You may find yourself nodding at everything I say and then a month from now find yourself failing to see any difference in your life. It could be that my examples only allowed you to think of others who need to hear this message, while you stayed safe because my examples didn't expose your own sin. I hope this is not the case. My hope and prayer is that this book will help to spur you on to create communities of people who long for a deep and intimate relationship with God. I hope that this may be the first step of many on a developmental journey into love.

This journey into love is the central concern for spiritual formation, and this book offers the first step toward a life of formation. Because I don't want to take you on a first step and then leave you to fend for yourself, I have helped to compile resources, tools, conversations, networks, and voices from the past for you to continue to grow and develop on the website www.metamorpha.com. This site, which was launched with my partner in ministry Jamin Goggin, exists so people can communally discuss the nature of spiritual transformation. For the issues in this book specifically, there will be some further information and resources on www.JesusAsAWayOfLife.com, for individual and group use. We hope that these various resources will prove to be an enlightening, developmental, and communal experience.

The vision I have for the journey ahead is for groups of people to enter together into the kind of life that is talked about in this book. I am more and more amazed at the opportunity we now have, for the first time in a long while, for unified developmental communities whose eyes are fixed on God and whose mission is the kingdom life now.

There comes a point when we are all called to be leaders simply because we have the ability to stop and decide to open ourselves honestly to God. The first steps in being honest with God should probably be saying, "I believe, help my unbelief," and starting or joining a community that says, "This is who we are, but by the grace of God it is not who we will remain."

Every generation in every context is called to find a place where all of the ideas in this book converge—the point of connection between all that we usually separate. It is only through the deconstructing work of the Spirit, through the Word, and within community that we will come to truly know ourselves and submit ourselves to the way of wisdom, which is the way of the cross. It is here that we find the intersection between the path of becoming and the work of mission in giving ourselves over to the hand of God.

The world was changed by a relatively small group of people who decided to take a journey with Christ two thousand years ago. They were given the Holy Spirit and a new family, and they had the words of Christ with them; in this sense they were in the same boat we are. And like us, they had a society around them full of people who thought they knew who Jesus was and what he was about. The world around them believed that all who followed Christ were fools, yet the early Christians were a bright light in the midst of the first century's darkness. Our mission is the same as theirs. They knew God, and because of this they grew to be like him and changed the world.

May we do the same.

NOTES

Chapter 1 Our Need

1. Cassie Blair, "Calcified Faith," *The Semi*, Fuller Theological Seminary, April 25–29, 2005, www.fuller.edu/student_life/SEMI/semi.asp.

2. "The reason why stories come into conflict with each other is that worldviews, and the stories which characterize them, are in principle *normative*: that is, they claim to make sense of the whole of reality." N. T. Wright, *The New Testament and the People of God* (Minneapolis: Fortress, 1992), 41.

3. C. S. Lewis, "Introduction," in *The Incarnation of the Word of God: Being the Treatise of St. Athanasius De Incarnatione Verbi Dei* (New York: Macmillan, 1947), 6–7.

4. James H. Olthuis, "On Worldviews," *Christian Scholars Review* 14, no. 2 (1985), http://www.gospel-culture.org.uk/olthuis.htm.

Chapter 2 Our Hope

1. This attitude that prefers whatever is comfortable for us can be clearly seen in how praise music has become such a huge issue in the church. The fact that there are church splits over music genre is proof that the church is in a very dark place. More often than not we are a people who seek out our own comfort, and that can even mean comfort in helping others, making them comfortable, etc. The means are irrelevant; the problem is that we care more about how we feel than whether we are growing.

2. The main problem with this word-picture is that the Spirit's role is put alongside community and the Bible, both of which need the Spirit to function well in the kingdom. The Spirit, as a member of the Trinity, must take precedence over the other two informers (at least ontologically). But since the Spirit has taken part in the creation of the Bible and has actually put himself under the authority of the Bible, the Bible takes precedence epistemically—in that we turn to the text for a more solid understanding of who the Spirit is, what he does, and how he relates before we turn to individual prayer as the authority on such matters. For the sake of clarification though, those issues will be addressed fully in a later chapter.

3. This example is precisely what Alvin Plantinga discusses in his work on proper function (see *Warranted Christian Belief* [New York : Oxford University Press, 2000]). It is not my purpose here to talk about proper function, but there is an interesting connection to what I am trying to do. The "path" that I am suggesting is a path for "proper functioning," and it helps to evaluate, critique, and guide our journey with God.

Chapter 3 Our Reality

1. Brian J. Walsh and J. Richard Middleton, *The Transforming Vision: Shaping a Christian World View* (Downers Grove, IL: InterVarsity, 1984), 17.

2. Through the book, I will refer to the task of "becoming." Typically, we talk about the difference between "doing" and "being," but I have been convinced by Dr. John Coe that this is the wrong way to look at it. The "doing"/"being" distinction makes sense, but the wording can be misleading. Our task is not necessarily one of being, but one of becoming. Our life is not one of arrival, as much as it is one of journey. Dr. John Coe is associate professor of philosophy and theology and director of the Institute for Spiritual Formation at Talbot School of Theology, La Mirada, California.

Chapter 4 The Word

1. At first glance, this is not that big of a problem. The Bible is one of the worldview informers that should be guiding our development. Yet without the other two informers offering discernment, it is easy to make any of the informers an end in and of themselves. Any of the informers taken alone will lead to a tainted form of Christianity. Even focusing on the Spirit will automatically lead to a maligned vision, because the Spirit works through the Word and community.

2. Anthony C. Thiselton, *New Horizons in Hermeneutics: The Theory and Practice of Transforming Biblical Reading* (Grand Rapids: Zondervan, 1992), 9.

3. "Revelation is thus not simply bridging of a noetic divide (though it includes that), but is reconciliation, salvation, and therefore fellowship. The idiom of revelation is as much moral and relational as it is cognitional." John Webster, *Holy Scripture: A Dogmatic Sketch*, Current Issues in Theology (Cambridge: Cambridge University Press, 2003), 16.

4. John Coe has helped me to put words to my experience of this reality as I went through seminary. Sadly, I have found few people who are open to admitting that seminary can be a course of study in puffing oneself up with a knowledge of the Bible.

5. Wright, *The New Testament and the People of God*, 81.

6. It is important to note that I am focusing entirely on a personal and ecclesiological reading of the text. I think it is hugely important to do serious background investigation for scholarly work and to focus solely on that kind of work. Christianity needs dedicated theologians, and their task, if done well, will build up the body of Christ and bless the community.

7. N. T. Wright, *Jesus and the Victory of God* (Minneapolis: Fortress, 1996), 175.

8. Ibid., 176.

9. K. R. Snodgrass, "Parable," in *Dictionary of Jesus and the Gospels*, ed. Joel G. Green, Scot McKnight, and I. Howard Marshall (Downers Grove, IL: InterVarsity, 1992), 597.

10. Anthony C. Thiselton, *The Two Horizons: New Testament Hermeneutics and Philosophical Description* (Grand Rapids: Eerdmans, 1980), 16.

11. "As God's free self-presentation, revelation is a *free work of sovereign mercy*. God's revelation is God's *spiritual* presence: God's is the personal subject of the act of revelation, and therefore revelation can in no way be commodified. God is—as Gerard Siegwalt puts it—revelation's 'uncontainable content'. As spiritual presence, the presence of God is free: it is not called forth by any reality other than itself; it is majestically spontaneous and uncaused. Its origin, actualization and accomplishment require nothing beyond God. Like the entire history of the divine mercy of which it is a part, revelation is unexpected, undeserved, possible only as and because God is, and present after the manner of God. In Barth's curious phrase, 'God is the Lord in the wording of His Word.'" Webster, *Holy Scripture*, 14–15.

12. Anthony Thiselton, "'Behind' and 'In Front of' the Text: Language, Reference and Indeterminacy," in *After Pentecost: Language and Biblical Interpretation*, ed. Craig Bartholomew, Colin Greene, and Karl Moller, Scripture and Hermeneutics Series (Grand Rapids: Zondervan, 2001), 98.

13. William Olhausen, "A 'Polite' Response to Anthony Thiselton," in *After Pentecost*, 128.

14. This idea was brought to fruition in my mind by John Coe, who has really helped me see the importance of "selfview" with the life of the Spirit. This inward engagement with the Word will also be dealt with more completely in the chapter on selfview.

15. It is interesting to note that God deems Jesus his Son when he is baptized: "A closer look at the way the 'Son of God' phrase is used shows that in [Mark] 1:11 the announcement reflects a combination of Ps. 2:7 and Isa. 42:1. What unites these allusions is the royal or kingly character and power of the one spoken about." Ben Witherington III, *The Gospel of Mark: A Socio-Rhetorical Commentary* (Grand Rapids: Eerdmans, 2001), 50.

16. D. R. Bauer makes the point that, while there is not a vast amount of literature in the Old Testament or ancient Judaism/Hellenism about the Son of God being the Messiah, two things are true: "(1) messianic hope in the period was almost always linked to an ideal Davidic king (who in the OT is described as Son of God) and (2) some NT statements seem to assume a connection between Messiah and Son of God." D. R. Bauer, "Son of God," in *Dictionary of Jesus and the Gospels*, 770. I personally think that this is a vast understatement, and the fact that the New Testament seems to assume a connection reveals the fact that this was an essential aspect of the Jewish worldview of the day.

17. Excerpt from the Chalcedonian Creed, quoted in Wayne Grudem, *Systematic Theology* (Grand Rapids: Zondervan, 1994), 1169.

18. William L. Lane, *The Gospel of Mark*, The New International Commentary on the New Testament (Grand Rapids: Eerdmans, 1974), 26.

19. R. T. France, *The Gospel of Mark*, The New International Greek Testament Commentary (Grand Rapids: Eerdmans, 2002), 16–17.

20. Michael J. Wilkins, *Following the Master: A Biblical Theology of Discipleship* (Grand Rapids: Zondervan, 1992), 196.

21. See the commentaries on Mark by R. T. France and William L. Lane.

22. For example, Geza Vermes states: "*Son of man* in Jewish Aramaic appears frequently as a synonym for 'man', and as a substitute for the indefinite pronoun; more seldom, as a circumlocution by which the speaker refers to himself." *Jesus the Jew: A Historian's Readings of the Gospels* (Philadelphia: Fortress, 1981), 176.

23. This was pointed out to me in discussion with Dr. Michael Wilkins, professor of New Testament language and literature and dean of the faculty, Talbot School of Theology.

24. Daniel 7 uses this language, but there wasn't any real expectation for the figure from Daniel 7 to come and be with the Jews. They were talking with the man Jesus and certainly weren't thinking about whether this guy was equal to God. The issue in Mark's Gospel was whether he was the Messiah, and only later is the divinity question brought up.

25. Larry W. Hurtado, "Following Jesus in the Gospel of Mark—and Beyond," in *Patterns of Discipleship in the New Testament*, ed. Richard N. Longenecker (Grand Rapids: Eerdmans, 1996), 27.

26. Michael Wilkins has pointed out to me how important it is to distinguish between these three groups of people. Jesus's message usually had to hit three different kinds of people: those who believed, those who were curious, and those who were adamantly opposed. These groups are representative for the way we read the text. Often we play the role of each group while reading a variety of texts.

27. John Coe, "A Theology of Intentional Character Formation" (unpublished manuscript, Institute for Spiritual Formation, Talbot School of Theology, La Mirada, California), 4, 10.

Chapter 5 The Spirit

1. John Coe has done more than anyone I know to really emphasize this point in his teaching, preaching, and writing, as well as to really work through the theological and personal implications of it.

2. Pope Leo XIII quoted in Stanley M. Burgess, *The Holy Spirit: Ancient Christian Traditions* (Peabody, MA: Hendrickson, 1984), 1.

3. R. A. Torrey, *The Person and Work of the Holy Spirit* (New York: Revell, 1910; repr. New Kensington, PA: Whitaker House, 1996), 7. Citation from the 1996 edition.

4. Robert Heidler, *Experiencing the Spirit: Developing a Living Relationship with the Holy Spirit* (Ventura, CA: Regal Books, 1998), 36.

5. Burgess, *The Holy Spirit*, 3.

6. Two men have helped me to see my lack of satisfaction in just being with God, both of whom find deep satisfaction in being with him: Wayne Anderson, who is the founder and director of Centering Ministries, and Paul Jensen, who is the executive director of the Leadership Institute.

7. Hilary of Poitiers quoted in Burgess, *The Holy Spirit*, 2.

8. Carlo Carretto, *The God Who Comes*, trans. Rose Mary Hancock (Maryknoll, NY: Orbis Books, 2001), 87.

9. More than anyone else, Michael Wilkins has helped me see the Jesus of the Gospels as well as the Jesus of history. His teaching has helped reintroduce me to Jesus and bring me to meet him on his terms and not mine.

10. This has also been pointed out by Michael Wilkins. As we know from Philippians 2, Jesus emptied himself and made himself nothing. While I think this has more to do with position and function, I think it still helps us understand Jesus's reliance upon the Spirit. We also see Jesus relying on the Spirit through prayer, solitude, silence, and other spiritual disciplines. Jesus did not do anything that another human did not do as well, other than forgive sins. This seems to be the one counterexample. Yet it seems that even the forgiving of sins had more to do with Jesus's position than with the fact that he was God.

11. It is a great temptation to try and change ourselves by what we do. This temptation is what John Coe calls the "moral temptation," which he talks about in a video on moral temptation at www.metamorpha.com.

12. Burgess, *The Holy Spirit*, 2.

13. Gary D. Badcock, *Light of Truth and Fire of Love: A Theology of the Holy Spirit* (Grand Rapids: Eerdmans, 1997), 257.

14. James Houston, *The Transforming Power of Prayer: Deepening Your Friendship with God* (Colorado Springs: NavPress, 1996), 69.

15. Clark Pinnock, *Flame of Love* (Downers Grove, IL: InterVarsity, 1996), 156.

16. Colin Gunton quoted in Jeff Imback, *The River Within: Loving God, Living Passionately* (Colorado Springs: NavPress, 1998), 66.

17. Gordon Fee, *God's Empowering Presence: The Holy Spirit in the Letters of Paul* (Peabody, MA: Hendrickson, 1994), 93.

18. Thomas R. Kelley quoted in Randall Harris, comp., *The Contemporaries Meet the Classics on the Holy Spirit* (West Monroe, LA: Howard Publishing, 2004), 124.

19. This is my simplistic way of saying that we should not allow the ontological (being) category to be determined by the epistemic (knowing) one.

20. I say this while thinking about miracles viewed from within this naturalistic context specifically. I have no doubt that in Africa and other areas where the worldview is more specifically "spiritual," these things make a much greater impact.

21. Quoted in Burgess, *The Holy Spirit*, 6–7.

Chapter 6 Community

1. The assumption here is that the fruit is actually good fruit, which is a pretty massive assumption, I know, but a necessary one for the time being.

2. Joseph H. Hellerman, *The Ancient Church as Family* (Minneapolis: Fortress, 2001), 70. This is the best book I have ever read on the ancient church. Dr. Hellerman is not only an incredible scholar, but he is a pastor with a pastor's heart. I had the opportunity to study under Joe at Talbot School of Theology and have come to really appreciate his love for the church as well as the ideology that drove the early church. I think his book is a must-read.

3. D. G. McCartney, "Household, Family," in *Dictionary of the Later New Testament and Its Development*, ed. Ralph P. Martin and Peter H. Davids (Downers Grove, IL: InterVarsity, 1997), 512.

4. Hellerman, *The Ancient Church as Family*, 29.

5. If you are up-to-date on the present conversation about first-century belief and how Jews understood their salvation in terms of "covenant nomism," to use E. P. Sander's term (see E. P. Sanders, *Paul and Palestinian Judaism: A Comparison of Patterns of Religion* (Minneapolis, MN: Fortress Press, 1977), then don't confuse that with the claim I am making here. I am merely trying to stay true to the text. Dr. Walt Russell, professor of Bible exposition, Talbot School of Theology, has helped me to see that these texts point toward an understanding of the bloodline of Abraham and their own self-understanding as children of the promises. That said, I have no doubt that the classical view of Pharisees and Jews is probably accurate as well. I just want to avoid making these ideas technical categories and then reading those back into the text.

6. C. J. H. Wright, "Family," *Anchor Bible Dictionary*, ed. David Noel Freedman (New York: Doubleday, 1992), 2:762.

7. McCartney, "Household, Family," in *Dictionary of the Later New Testament and Its Development*, 513.

8. Seneca, *Letters from a Stoic*, trans. Robin Campbell (New York: Penguin Books, 1969), 50.

9. J. Ramsey Michaels, "Going to Heaven with Jesus: From 1 Peter to Pilgrim's Progress," in *Patterns of Discipleship in the New Testament*, ed. Richard N. Longenecker (Grand Rapids: Eerdmans, 1996), 267.

10. Jean Vanier, *Community and Growth*, 2nd ed. (New York: Paulist Press, 1989), 26–27.

11. Most translations will actually translate this "gentle," which is unusual because every commentator I have read admits that this is not the word in the Greek. There is only one letter difference between *infant* and *gentle* in Greek, and it seems that some of the later manuscripts have changed the word *infant* to *gentle*. The likely scenario is that a scribe accidentally messed up the word, or else he didn't like Paul referring to himself as an infant. If the latter is true, then that mistake is a prime example of one's worldview getting in the way of one's theology.

12. Most translations render this something other than "orphaned," even though the word does in fact mean "to be orphaned," failing to take seriously that Paul is using family terminology abundantly throughout this section to show his love and connection with the Thessalonians. See Jeffrey A. D. Weima, "But We Became Infants Among You: The Case for NHPIOI in 1 Thess 2.7," *New Testament Studies* 46 (2000): 547–64.

13. Vanier, *Community and Growth*, 19.

14. Webster, *Holy Scripture*, 46–47.

15. In the initial draft of this section, I had narrowed *tribe* to just North American Christians, hoping to show how we in North America can help form each other—but we are so divided that the section would have been basically meaningless. I didn't want to jump from town to world so quickly, but I think that the overall point comes across regardless.

16. Vanier, *Community and Growth*, 16–17.

17. This idea was derived from either one of two sources: (1) my good friend Walt Russell or (2) the Chinese food that we were eating. Although, as I recall, it may have been a good combination of both.

18. George M. Marsden, *Jonathan Edwards: A Life* (London: Yale University Press, 2003), 337.

19. My professor John Coe has helped me to see how true this in fact is.

20. James Houston, *The Transforming Power of Prayer*, 238.

21. Diognetus quoted in Tim Dowley, ed., *Introduction to the History of Christianity* (Minneapolis: Fortress, 1995), 67.

Chapter 7 Selfview

1. John Calvin, *Institutes of the Christian Religion*, ed. John T. McNeill (Philadelphia: Westminster, 1960), 35. John Coe first pointed out this quote to me, as well as the noteworthy fact that Calvin starts his *Institutes* this way.

2. Clement of Alexandria quoted in Alexander Roberts, James Donaldson, and A. Cleveland Coxe, *The Ante-Nicene Fathers*, vol. 2, *Translations of the Writings of the Fathers Down to A.D. 325* (Oak Harbor, WA: Logos Research Systems, 1997), 271.

3. Martin Luther quoted in James M. Houston, "The 'Double Knowledge' as the Way of Wisdom," in *The Way of Wisdom: Essays in Honor of Bruce K. Waltke*, ed. J. I. Packer and Sven K. Soderlund (Grand Rapids: Zondervan, 2000), 316.

4. John Coe was the first to introduce me to this idea. John has made the important point many times that we start our Christian life in conversion at the foot of the cross, and that often becomes the last time we are ever there. But for true growth, we need to grow from the same place that we first met Christ, when He was sufficient and we were totally unable.

5. Houston, "The 'Double Knowledge,' " 321.

6. Dallas Willard, "The Human Disaster of Unbelief," in audiotape lectures *Living an Eternal Life Now* (Chatsworth, CA: The Sower's Yield, Tape Division, n.d.).

7. Certainly there are many other beliefs that could come into this discussion, such as: money is evil, having that much money would be more problematic than it is worth, etc.

8. See J. P. Moreland, *Love Your God With All Your Mind: The Role of Reason in the Life of the Soul* (Colorado Springs: NavPress, 1997), 73–77.

9. Ibid.

10. Much of my thinking on the deep belief structures we have that guide our behavior has been formed by Karen Horney, *Neurosis and Human Growth: The Struggle Toward Self-Realization* (New York: W. W. Norton, 1950).

11. I first heard John Coe state this about something else, but it seems to apply here as well.

12. *The Shawshank Redemption*, written by Stephen King and Frank Darabont, directed by Frank Darabont (Columbia Pictures, 1994).

13. William Barclay quoted in Simon Chan, *Spiritual Theology: A Systematic Study of the Christian Life* (Downers Grove, IL: InterVarsity, 1998), 153.

14. David G. Benner, *Surrender to Love: Discovering the Heart of Christian Spirituality* (Downers Grove, IL: InterVarsity, 2003), 15.

15. A. W. Tozer, *The Knowledge of the Holy* (San Francisco: HarperSanFrancisco, 1961), 1.

16. There have been many people who have mirrored this reality back to me lately, but the one who continues to do so has been Jamin Goggin, my partner at www.metamorpha. com, and my close friend. I continue to see how much my love of ideas has formed the way I see reality, and I appreciate the reminder that my ways are not God's.

17. My friend John Coe has shown me, through the ancient spiritualists, how the task of spiritual formation is this way as well: that any kind of real growth is cyclical in nature and not progressive. He has also shown me how fleshly the desire for constant growth is. It is truly seeing things according to man's way and neglecting God's.

18. Thomas H. Green, SJ, *Weeds among the Wheat: Discernment, Where Prayer and Action Meet* (Notre Dame, IN: Ave Maria Press, 1970), 59.

19. Tozer, *Knowledge of the Holy*, 4.

20. Thiselton, *New Horizons in Hermeneutics*, 14.

21. Thomas H. Green, SJ, *Opening to God: A Guide to Prayer* (Notre Dame, IN: Ave Maria Press, 1977), 81.

22. John Coe has helped me to understand what it really means to have those deep beliefs about God and his world changed. Before he helped me to understand a more formational model of development, I did in fact try to discern what I truly believed, but only in a rough and confused way. He has helped me to see that we need to sit in the reality of who we are so that God can open us up to the work that his Spirit is doing in our hearts. Our task is to be open to this work of the Spirit in all things, particularly in

the realization we will have that we tend not to believe as we ought to believe. Without John, I would probably still be struggling through much of my brokenness, and for his assistance and guidance I will be eternally grateful.

23. Green, *Weeds among the Wheat*, 155.

24. I think I first heard this said by Dallas Willard, although I can't remember where or when. What I think may be more interesting about the story of Jesus's temptation is whether or not Jesus saw Satan. I have often thought about Jesus seeing this great big guy with a pitchfork, but I imagine that probably didn't happen. It seems then that Jesus was discerning enough to be able to perceive what was the Spirit of God speaking inside of him and what was Satan. This task is relatively ignored today, and it seems that it should be taken very seriously.

25. Chan, *Spiritual Theology*, 154.

26. Ibid., 153.

27. Green, *Opening to God*, 82.

28. More than anyone else, John Coe has shown me how feeling better is the motivation for most of what we do. I am constantly amazed at how much I do because I want to feel better, and so I confess, read my Bible, or just do something "Christian" to feel better. That is a vicious, self-centered cycle.

29. Karl Barth, *The Church and the Churches* (Grand Rapids: Eerdmans, 2005), 30.

30. Augustine quoted in Chan, *Spiritual Theology*, 153.

31. Jonathan Edwards quoted in Marsden, *Jonathan Edwards*, 45.

32. Jeffrey H. Boyd, "One's Self-Concept and Biblical Theology," *Journal of the Evangelical Theological Society* 40, no. 2 (June 1997): 208.

Chapter 8 Wisdom

1. Daniel J. Estes, *Hear, My Son: Teaching and Learning in Proverbs 1–9*, New Studies in Biblical Theology (Grand Rapids: Eerdmans, 1997), 28–29. There is a great discussion in this section of Estes's work that helps to separate the biblical proverb from the ancient Egyptian concept of *Maat*.

2. I have become convinced of this view of Ecclesiastes because of the very wise Edward Curtis, who was both an incredible Hebrew teacher and a guide whose wisdom seems endless. He has a great discussion of Ecclesiastes in his book: Edward M. Curtis and John J. Brugaletta, *Discovering the Ways of Wisdom: Spirituality in the Wisdom Literature* (Grand Rapids: Kregel, 2004), 192–212. John Coe was the first to open me up to a more metalevel understanding of the wisdom literature in this way. After reflecting upon this, I believe it to have much merit and to be very helpful in understanding the worldview in which the earliest believers were a part.

3. Estes, *Hear, My Son*, 45.

4. Ibid , 50.

5. Gerhard Von Rad, *Wisdom in Israel* (London: Trinity Press International, 1970), 66.

6. Ibid.

7. John of the Cross quoted in Kieran Kavanaugh, OCD, *John of the Cross: Doctor of Light and Love* (New York: Crossroad, 1999), 113.

8. Estes, *Hear, My Son*, 27.

9. C. S. Lewis, *The Weight of Glory: And Other Addresses* (San Francisco: HarperSanFrancisco, 1976), 54.

10. Curtis and Brugaletta, *Discovering the Ways of Wisdom*, 48.

11. Ibid. (translation by Curtis). I would like to thank Dr. Ed Curtis, professor of Old Testament, Talbot School of Theology, for pointing this out as a good example to use.

12. Quotation originally used in reference to Proverbs 2:1–5 in Derek Kidner, *Proverbs*, vol. 15, Tyndale Old Testament Commentaries (Downers Grove, IL: InterVarsity, 1964), 61. This was quoted in and adapted in Curtis and Brugaletta, *Discovering the Ways of Wisdom*, 204, in talking about Ecclesiastes. As is clear from the quote, although Kidner was speaking of Proverbs specifically, his insights apply to all of the wisdom literature.

13. Fee, *God's Empowering Presence*, 93.

14. I've heard this idea numerous times from Dallas Willard in his lectures.

15. Lawrence Toombs, "Old Testament Theology and the Wisdom Literature," *Journal of Bible and Religion* 23 (1955): 194–95.

Chapter 9 The Way of Jesus

1. From the movie *Billy Madison*, written by Tim Herlihy and Adam Sandler, directed by Tamara Davis (Universal Pictures, 1995). When I was in high school I saw this movie probably more than any other, and this scene is what has stuck in my mind. It lives out, better than most movies I have seen, what Philippians 2 is talking about.

2. I believe this interpretation was first suggested to me in conversation with J. P. Moreland, distinguished professor of philosophy, Talbot School of Theology.

3. Neil Elliott, *Liberating Paul: The Justice of God and the Politics of the Apostle* (Maryknoll, NY: Orbis Books, 1994), 93, quoted in Michael J. Gorman, *Cruciformity: Paul's Narrative Spirituality of the Cross* (Grand Rapids: Eerdmans, 2001), 5, 17. I highly recommend reading Gorman's book, which is an excellent analysis that is both readable and expansive.

4. Gorman, *Cruciformity*, 14.

5. I am adapting this treatment of Paul's and Jesus's résumé from the work a friend of mine has done on Philippians. For an excellent and extremely in-depth treatment of this subject, please read Joseph H. Hellerman, *Reconstructing Honor in Roman Philippi: Carmen Christi as Cursus Pudorum*, Society for New Testament Studies Monograph Series (Cambridge: Cambridge University Press, 2005).

6. "'Sanctification' is a process of both life and death; death is working in the believer as well as life. This is the consequence of his divided state: although as a member of the last Adam, as belonging to Christ through the Spirit, he is living; at the same time, as a member of the first Adam, as belonging to the world as flesh, he is dying. A particular expression of this is the suffering of the believer." James D. G. Dunn, *Jesus and the Spirit: A Study of the Religious and Charismatic Experience of Jesus and the First Christians as Reflected in the New Testament* (Grand Rapids: Eerdmans, 1975), 327.

7. It is not the place to go into this here, nor am I able to talk about this with any sort of expertise, but this "blindness" would correspond to John of the Cross's idea of the dark night, as well as the anonymous work from the fourteenth century, *The Cloud of Unknowing*.

8. The discussion of these types of narratives is broad and deep, but I wanted to offer one in particular, simply because it is from an interesting source. See the chapter "Walking to Emmaus in a Postmodern World" in N. T. Wright, *The Challenge of Jesus: Rediscovering Who Jesus Was and Is* (Downers Grove, IL: InterVarsity, 1999).

9. Dunn, *Jesus and the Spirit*, 331.

10. This conversation was from a class discussion, and my responses were mostly in my head (unspoken). The friend is Edward Curtis, who is an amazingly wise man of faith.

11. There were certainly many times when Abraham seemed to live according to the reality he saw, but the tenor of his life was one lived by faith.

12. Allen P. Ross, *Creation and Blessing: A Guide to the Study and Exposition of Genesis* (Grand Rapids: Baker, 1998), 281.

13. I know that the first time this thought was suggested to me was by Dallas Willard, although I do not recall if it was in a book or from a lecture.

Chapter 10 Discipleship

1. Eugene Peterson, *The Wisdom of Each Other* (Grand Rapids: Zondervan, 2001), 42.

2. My good friend Walt Russell pointed this out to me, and the remainder of this section is a reflection of what Walt has been in my life—a brother who has helped guide, mentor, and walk with me along the way. He was the first to point me to community as being my fellow disciples who, through the Spirit's work in and through their lives, help to form me into a disciple. It is amazing how many programs are developed that only give "mature" Christians their own little group of disciples. They put themselves in the same place where Jesus was, but without his understanding, grace, or ability to teach. In the end, most of these disciples merely end up mimicking the person they follow, without being helped to know Jesus in deeper ways.

3. Wilkins, *Following the Master*, 353.

4. Ibid., 354.

5. Michael Wilkins was the first to open my eyes to how inadequate a definition the metaphor of apprenticeship really is for discipleship.

6. Jesus was certainly a teacher, but to treat him solely as a mere teacher would be a gross understatement.

7. Ana-Maria Rizzuto, MD, *The Birth of the Living God: A Psychoanalytic Study* (Chicago: University of Chicago Press, 1979), 8.

8. Calvin, *Institutes of the Christian Religion*, 37.

9. Michael Wilkins makes this point adamantly, which is why he thinks the term *apprentice* fails to capture the reality of the disciple.

10. While a lot of commentators have noted this, N. T. Wright hammers home this particular viewpoint of Jesus (a prophet) in his trilogy of books discussing the historical Jesus. The second volume, *Jesus and the Victory of God*, is a good read towards this end.

Chapter 11 Mission

1. Dallas Willard makes this point abundantly clear in his excellent book *The Divine Conspiracy: Rediscovering Our Hidden Life in God* (San Francisco: HarperSanFrancisco, 1998).

2. The idea of using this principle came from a member of the group who was slightly obsessed with the movie *Fight Club*. There is an interesting parallel in this movie to the kingdom, although it might better show what happens when things are done man's way over God's way! Nonetheless, I think the lesson we learned was an important one.

3. Lesslie Newbigin, *The Gospel in a Pluralistic Society* (Grand Rapids: Eerdmans, 1989), 119, emphasis added.

4. Ibid.

5. My friend John Coe has helped me to see the implications of this theologically and, more importantly, personally. This is why it is imperative to have an adequate understanding of ourselves, that we may truly come to be with God as we really are and not as we wish we were.

6. Michael Wilkins has helped me to see the implications of Jesus's message to the crowds, as well as how important it is to learn from Jesus's method as we approach spiritual seekers as well.

7. Moyer Hubbard, *2 Corinthians*, vol. 3, Zondervan Illustrated Bible Backgrounds Commentary, ed. Clinton E. Arnold (Grand Rapids: Zondervan, 2002), 207, emphasis added.

8. Ibid.

9. Ibid.

10. Newbigin, *The Gospel in a Pluralistic Society*, 119.

11. G. K. Chesteron, *What's Wrong with the World* (New York: Cassell, 1910), chapter 5; or online at the American Chesterton Society, http://www.chesterton.org/discover/quotations.html.

Kyle Strobel is a speaker, writer, and practitioner of spiritual formation, discipleship, and community transformation. He has a BA in biblical studies, an MA in philosophy of religion and ethics, and an MA in New Testament from Talbot School of Theology. After doing further graduate work in spiritual formation, Kyle has started his PhD in theology at the University of Aberdeen in Scotland, where he and his wife, Kelli, currently reside. Kyle is also cofounder and director of www.metamorpha.com, an online community for spiritual formation.

For more great resources, visit www.metamorpha.com

Metamorpha.com exists to foster community among people who want to grow in their relationship with Christ. The site offers educational tools and methods, as well as opportunities for communal interaction, retreats, spiritual direction, group prayer, and reading exercises.

In addition, Metamorpha.com is a professional resource: for pastors, to help them live and lead in a healthy and growing way; for churches, to help them take on an educational and consulting role in creating communities of people growing in Christ; and for individuals who are on a journey with Christ, to encourage, guide, and nurture growth in their lives.